EQUITY INVESTING

Wealth Creation Strategies

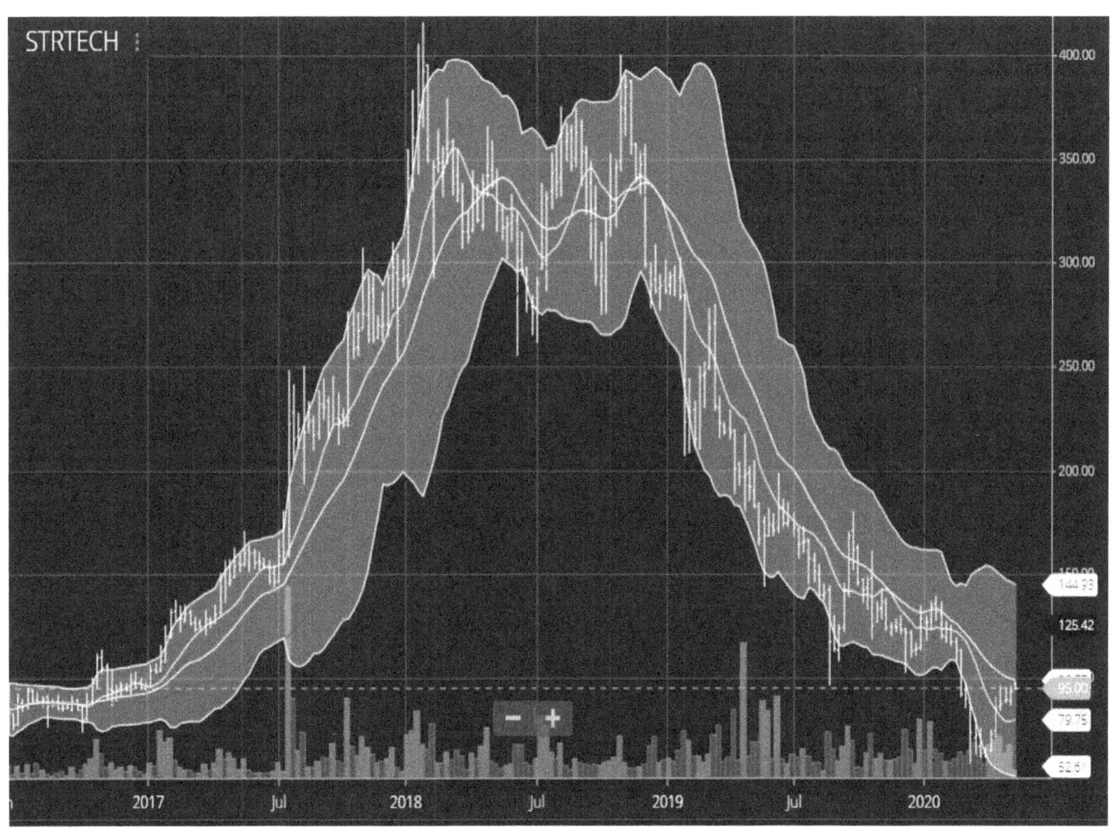

Dr V.K. Jain

TABLE OF CONTENTS

----------oooooooo---------

Chapter 1

INTRODUCTION

"Wealth is unmatched beauty, wealth is auspicious, wealth is bursting youth, wealth is life itself"
- Chankya

1.1 Why Equity?

Equity refers to the amount of capital contributed by the owners. In other words, equity represents the ownership stake in a company. The term share is slightly different; shares are the measurement of the ownership proportion of the individual in the company. In general both the terms equity and share are used interchangeably. The terms equity market and stock market also have the same meaning. The lure of stock markets attracts many investors and common men. But investing in equity or stocks is not one way terrain. The market moves up, down or sideways and may remain there for a long time. The stock market is volatile as it ii is sensitive to local and global economy and political news. When you follow hot tips from friends, brokers and advice from TV experts, you buy shares of a company and hold it for long. You ultimately find that the stock is going no where or it is going southwards. You still do not sell it hoping that it will bounce back soon and recover the loss. This is how you destroy wealth rather than creating it. It is therefore imperative to invest in equity sensibly. This calls for right selection of stock(s), entry and exit strategies.

Out of the many investment avenues, investing in stocks promises great returns. Historically equity investing has delivered highest returns over the long-term as compared to any other asset class. But only 3% of our country's population buys stocks. Of these very few people invest in shares, that is, hold shares for medium or long term, most of them are speculators or traders who ride the short term momentum in stock prices and sell the shares as the target is met or book the loss if the stock price takes opposite turn. Traders sometime gain and more often lose, they seldom make money. It requires a lot of diligence, control of emotions and money management to succeed in trading. An investor on the contrary buys stocks of good business at the right time, holds them with longer perspective. He reviews his portfolio periodically, may be weekly, monthly or yearly and exits the stock when the business of the company goes soar. There are many wonderful businesses having sound fundamentals and reasonable predictable future earnings. Identification of such businesses and investing in them at the right time can unlock your fortune. There are Multibagger stocks which multiply their price by tens, even hundreds of times. There are companies which build wide and strong moats to create a barrier to competition. Warren Buffet, the biggest investor of our times terms these companies, moat companies. Multibagger stocks are discussed in another chapter. Following right stock selection with good business and predictable future earnings, entry and exit strategies, one can create wealth over the long term. This book attempts to describe these strategies in detail along with numerous examples from the Indian stock market.

As described above equity is the best investment option in the long term. You should invest a considerable portion of savings in equity for long term wealth creation. The following paragraphs list advantages of investing in equities.

(1) Hedge against inflation: Equities stand out against other asset classes in outpacing inflation over the long term. Investing in equities is similar to investing in a business. Since strong businesses have the ability to pass on inflation and thus increase their product prices to negate its impact, equities have the potential to absorb inflation over the long term.

(2) Long-term growth potential: History clearly shows that only two asset classes have grown faster than inflation over decades, real estate and common stock (shares or equity). Equity is the best asset class for creating long-term wealth. If a strong business, which is growing and has good return ratios, is bought at an early stage of growth and at cheap valuations, the long-term wealth creation can be phenomenal. For example, investors who invested in the Infosys IPO in 1993 would have multiplied their wealth by over 3000 times over the past 20 years. Stock market has given an average return of about 10-13% over the decades. Small company stocks have grown more than blue chip (large, well-established and financially sound company) stocks albeit with much greater volatility.

(3) Liquidity: Stocks of listed companies are one of the easiest types of assets to liquidate if cash is needed. They can be sold on stock exchanges and cash can be obtained in 3 days.

(4) Wide variety: Stocks come in a large variety from large cap to small cap, growth, value, high dividend yield, sectoral and cyclical etc. One can select stocks to suit his/ her need and behaviour.

(5) Availability of vast information: Wealth of information about the performance and profitability of public listed companies is freely available in media, on stock exchange websites, company's prospectus etc., bringing transparency and settling its price to correct value.

(6) Dividend income: Stocks of good companies pay a periodic dividend to investors. Some stocks pay high dividends and are suitable for investors seeking income, while others pay little or no dividend but post strong capital gains.

(7) Tax exemption: In present tax laws long term capital gain upto Rs1 lakh from sale of shares is exempt from income tax, if held for more than one year. Long term capital gain above Rs1 lakh is charged at 10%.   Short term capital gain is taxed at a concessional rate of 15%. Dividend income is completely exempt from tax. It makes investment in equities tax efficient.

To summarise the rewards of investing in equity are hedge against inflation, long term wealth creation, diversification , regular dividend income, liquidity, scope of capital appreciation by way of rise of market price, issue of bonus and right shares, hassle free buy or sale transactions on Internet or phone from the convenience of home. Not participating in the stock markets during the growth phase can be considered as an opportunity missed. Growth brings inflation, which drives up the cost of living and eats away at the value of savings. You need to stay invested in high-growth asset classes to beat inflationary pressures. In fact investors of blue chip, moat companies or good stocks have been handsomely rewarded. The following paragraphs describe a few such stocks.

Types of shares

There are two main types of stocks, common and preferred. The main distinction between the two is that common shares carry voting rights in the annual general meeting (AGM) in matters such as election of Directors while preferred shares generally do not have voting rights. Preferred shares have preference over the common shares in a company to receive dividends as well as assets in the event of liquidation. Most of the shares issued by a company are common shares. In general we mean common shares by the term equity or shares.

Stock Exchanges

Stock markets consist of Primary and Secondary markets. Primary market is a place where companies issue shares and bonds initially to the public by Initial Public Offerings (IPOs). Once these shares or bonds are issued, these can be bought or sold in secondary markets or Stock Exchanges. In other words new shares are issued in primary market by IPO and traded in secondary market or stock exchanges. Today's stock exchanges are electronic where trading takes place in fraction of a second when Ask for (what sellers are willing to take) and Bid price (the price buyers are willing to pay) match. There are two major stock exchanges in India, viz., Bombay Stock Exchange (BSE) and National Stock Exchange (NSE). Most of the trading in the Indian stock market takes place on its two stock exchanges. Almost all the significant firms of India are listed on both the exchanges. As BSE has 5,518 listed firms, whereas the rival NSE has about 1,795.. Out of all the listed firms on the BSE, only about 500 firms constitute more than 90% of its market capitalization; the rest of the stocks are highly illiquid.

Stock Market Indices

A Stock Market Index is a method of measuring performance of certain group of stocks of a stock market. Their performance shows how the overall market economy or a particular industry is. There are following major stock market indices in India: BSE Sensex and Nifty 50. BSE Sensex 30 is weighted average of 30 stocks having the highest free float market capitalisation whereas Nifty 50 is a little broader market index of top 50 stocks. BSE Sensex is very sensitive to price fluctuations of large cap companies. These are the most popular indices. Broad based indices are BSE 100, BSE 200, BSE 500, Nifty 100, Nifty 200 and Nifty 500. BSE Indices based on market capitalisation are BSE Large cap, Mid cap and Small cap. NSE indices based on market capitalisation are NIFTY 100, NIFTY Midcap 150, NIFTY Small cap 250. Besides there are host of sectoral indices like BSE Finance, BSE Healthcare, Nifty Auto, Nifty Bank etc.

Classification of Companies

According to market capitalisation, companies are classified as Large cap, Mid cap and Small cap. Market capitalisation refers to total Rupee value of a company's outstanding shares. It is calculated by multiplying the total number of company's outstanding shares by the current market price of one share. Companies with a market cap of more than Rs10,000 crore are classified as large cap, those with market cap between Rs500 crore and Rs10,000 crore are called mid cap companies. Remaining companies with market cap less than Rs500 crore are called small cap companies. Their important characteristics are:

Parameters	Large cap	Mid cap	Small cap
Risk involved	Low	High	Very high
Return expectation	Low	High	Very high
Liquidity	High	High	Low
Funds's holding	High	Medium	Low
Availability of information	Very high	High	Low

Price Variation

Stock prices change every day as a result of market forces. The stock price moves up and down in short spells due to traders who are speculators - the short term players. In actively traded shares there are big intraday moves. By this, we mean that share prices change because of supply and demand. If more people want to buy a stock (demand) than sell it (supply), then the price moves up. Conversely, if more people wanted to sell a stock than buy it, there would be greater supply than demand, and the price would fall.

The most important factor that affects the value of a company is its earnings. Earnings are the profit a company makes, and in the long run no company can survive without them. Analysts base future value of a company on its earnings projection. If a company's results are better than expected, the price jumps up. If a company's results are worse than expected, then the price will fall. Of course, it's not just earnings that can change the sentiment towards a stock. As discussed above, the stock price variation to a large extent depends on investor psychology. These are driven by company, industry and political news, global clues, rumors, investor's perception about future earning, growth of the stock etc. Many theories and mathematical models are in vogue to predict the future price of stocks but none is really complete and trustworthy. That is why technical analysts believe that price is everything and they watch movement of price very closely.

Buying and Selling Shares

Listed shares on any of the recognized stock exchange can only be bought or sold through its brokers. Transacting a share involves the following steps:

1. *Locating a broker:* You can locate a broker member of the stock exchange from the advertisements or from your friends investing in share market. Some leading online brokers are listed in Appendix II. You will have to submit a client registration form and a member-constituent form for order/ trade confirmation, brokerage charged and delivery of securities or funds.

2. *Placing an order(s):* After completing preliminaries you can place buy or sell order at market or limit order rates. Market rate order will be executed immediately at the prevailing market price. Limit order puts a constraint on sale or purchase of the share, the sale will not be affected below the limit order price and in case of purchase, purchase will not be made above limit order price. Limit orders are valid only for the day.

3. *Execution of order:* Once the buy / sell order is executed, the broker will confirm the order, handover you the contact note and will expect the payment (in case of buy order) and delivery slip

(in case of sell order). Delivery slip is like cheque book issued to you at the time of opening the account with the broker.

Online Trading

Most of the brokers have gone online at present. You can buy / sell shares online from the convenience of your home without any human intervention. For this you will have to trade with a broker who can provide a trading terminal at your home (Refer to Annexure II for a partial list of such brokers). Almost all big broking houses provide 3-in-1 account allowing maintenance of demat (dematerialized) shares, trading and payment, all at one place. Your home PC or laptop or even smart phone can act as broker terminal with just an Internet connection. Limit orders, valid for the day, may also be placed. Both way payments can be made through bank gateways making the entire trade paperless.

Many brokers provide stock rates and even intraday charts on your mobile enabling you to track and trade your stocks from anywhere, even while on move. In fact you can watch intraday chart of the share you wish to trade and execute the trade at the best possible rate. Besides you can make online technical analysis for better buy and sell decisions. Almost all broking houses provide trading tips and investment advice to the naïve investors, though their accuracy is a question mark. Many free websites viz., www.moneycontrol.com, www.finwance.yahoo.com, www.google.com/fiannce, www. bseindia.com, www.nseindia.com, www.etportfolio.com, www.in.investing.com etc. provide intraday and daily technical charts along with fundamental analysis. For a detailed list refer to Appendix I.

Advanced analysis of stocks can also be made by many stock softwares like e-signal, Metastock, investing.com, marketsmith.com, marketsmojo.com etc. By use of expert systems buy and sell decisions can even be automated. These systems can even trigger a sell decision in case of a steep market fall and make a call to the broker thus protecting your gains and capital in case of an unprecedented steep fall triggered by a bad domestic or international economic or political event thus saving you from the slaughter of the stock market.

Algorithmic trading, also called algo or robo trading, is gaining popularity now a days among institutional investors. It uses a computer program that follows a set of predefined instructions (programme) based on timing, price, quantity to place a trade. It can execute thousands of small trades in a day which cannot be matched by a human trader. Some brokers like Zerodha.com allow retail investors to go for algo trading. The investors can either choose readymade programmes or write their own programmes in simple scripting language. These formulae or programmes can be back tested over a pretty long period and thus the best trading formula can be applied to a specific stock.

1.4 Historical Sensex Returns

As mentioned above equity as an asset class has delivered best returns in the long term. The following table shows historical annual, 5 year and 10 year Sensex rolling returns.

Table - Sensex Historical Rolling Returns

Sensex Annual Returns	Sensex 5 Years Rolling Returns	Sensex 10 Years Rolling Returns

Year	Sensex*	Annual Return	Year ending	Sensex*	5 Year Return#	Year ending	Sensex*	10 Year Return#
2009	9,709	-38%	2009	9,709	12%	2009	9,709	10%
2010	17,528	81%	2010	17,528	22%	2010	17,528	13%
2011	19,445	11%	2011	19,445	12%	2011	19,445	18%
2012	17,404	-10%	2012	17,404	6%	2012	17,404	18%
2013	18,836	8%	2013	18,836	4%	2013	18,836	20%
2014	22,386	19%	2014	22,386	18%	2014	22,386	15%
2015	27,957	25%	2015	27,957	10%	2015	27,957	16%
2016	25,342	-9%	2016	25,342	5%	2016	25,342	8%
2017	29,621	17%	2017	29,621	11%	2017	29,621	9%
2018	32,969	11%	2018	32,969	12%	2018	32,969	8%
2019	38,673	17%	2019	38,673	12%	2019	38,673	15%
Note *	Closing index values as on last trading day of March							
#	Sensex historical 5, 10 years rolling return is compound annual growth return (CAGR).							

[Source: https://kunaldesai.blog/sensex-returns/]

The above table demonstrates that 10 year Sensex rolling returns vary from 8% to 20%, higher than bonds or bank fixed deposits. This is the case of passive investing, that is, buying Sensex as a whole. With active investing the returns will be much higher. This again proves superiority of equity investing over other asset classes.

1.5 Fundamental Analysis

Fundamental analysis techniques include macroeconomic factors such as global, national, and industrial outlooks, interest rates, and inflation. An investor ultimately invests his/ her money in the shares of one or more companies with the objective of dividend income and capital appreciation. Each company belongs to an industry. Performance of a company would be influenced by the fortunes of the industry to which it belongs. For this reason an investor must study the industry in which he/ she is investing. Health of various industries can be gauged by BSE sectoral indices like Oil and Gas, FMCG, Metal, Bankex, PSU, Consumer Durables, Capital Goods, Healthcare, Auto, Realty, Tech, IT and Power. Depending on the country's economic conditions some sectors outperform than others. Every industry goes through different   stages of a life cycle. These stages are: (a) Pioneering stage, (b) Expansion stage, (c) Stagnation stage and (d) Decay stage. The first step in analysis of an industry is, therefore, to determine the stage of growth through which the industry is passing. After deciding which industry to invest in, you will need to select a company(s). In analysis/ selection of a company both qualitative and quantitative factors are important. These are described in brief below:

(1) Qualitative Analysis

Qualitative factors in a company analysis include the following: Business Model, Competitive Advantage, Management, Corporate Governance, quality of a company's board members and key executives, its brand-name recognition, patents or proprietary technology.

(2) Quantitative Analysis

Quantitative analysis measures the current performance and forecasts the future performance in numerical terms. The biggest source of quantitative data is the financial statement. Through it you can measure revenue, profit, assets and more with great precision.

Financial Statement: Financial statements are the medium by which a company discloses information concerning its financial performance. The main financial statements are:

- Balance Sheet: The balance sheet represents a record of a company's assets, liabilities and equity at a particular point in time. As the name suggests, balance sheet balances the equation:
- Assets = Liabilities + shareholders' equity.

Assets represent the resources that the business owns or controls at a given point in time. This includes items such as cash, inventory, machinery and buildings. Liabilities represent debt, while equity represents the total value of money that the owners have contributed to the business - including retained earnings, which is the profit made in previous years. While the balance sheet takes a snapshot approach in examining a business, the income statement measures a company's performance over a specific time frame such quarterly or annually. The income statement gives information about revenues, expenses and profit for the specified period. The cash flow statement represents a record of a business' cash inflows and outflows over the specified period. It includes operating cash flow, that is, cash generated from day-to-day operations, cash from investing and cash from financing. Some investors use the cash flow statement as a more conservative measure of a company's performance, as it is tough to manipulate cash with the bank.

Key Ratios

Performance of a company can be measured by the following terms and ratios. Ratios make comparison of performance of two or more companies easy. Broadly the ratios can be classified into the following categories:

(i) Liquidity
(ii) Solvency
(iii) Profitability
(iv) Activity

(i) Liquidity Ratios

Liquidity ratios also called working capital or short term solvency ratios are divided in the following sub categories:

Current Ratio: It is an indicator of a firm's commitment to meet its short term liabilities. It is the ratio of Current Assets to Current Liabilities. Current assets are cash or assets that can easily be converted into cash within a year or operating cycle which is longer. Current assets are used to fund day-to-day operations and pay ongoing expenses. Cash is the most liquid current asset. Marketable securities can be easily converted into cash but inventory is the most illiquid asset. Current liabilities are payables within one year or operating cycle which is longer.

Quick Ratio: Also called Acid Test Ratio, is the ratio of Quick Assets to Current Liabilities. Quick assets are the current assets less inventory and prepaid expenses. Standard value of Quick Ratio is 1:1, which means that the cash yield from the most liquid assets is sufficient to pay off short term liabilities.

Working Capital Turnover Ratio: It is the ratio of Net Sales to Net Working Capital. It is also called Liquid Surplus, that is, excess of liquidity. Too high value of this ratio indicates inefficient utilization of funds and vice-versa.

(ii) Solvency Ratios

These ratios ascertain the long term solvency of a company, which depends on the following factors: (i) adequacy to meet long term fund requirements, (b) appropriate debt-equity mix to raise long term funds, and (iii) adequacy of earnings to pay interest and installment of long term loan. These ratios are subdivided in the following ratios:

Debt: Equity Ratio: Debt / equity ratio is a measure of a company's financial leverage calculated by dividing its total liabilities by stockholders' equity. It indicates what proportion of equity and debt the company is using to finance its assets. A high debt/equity ratio generally means that a company has been aggressive in financing its growth with debt. This can result in reduced earnings as a result of the additional interest expense. The debt/equity ratio also depends on the industry in which the company operates, e.g., capital-intensive industries such as auto manufacturing tend to have a debt/equity ratio above 2, while IT companies have a low debt/equity of under 0.5.

Fixed Assets Ratio: It is the ratio of Net Fixed Assets to Long Term Debts. It indicates the sufficiency of the value of fixed assets to cover the amount of the long term loan. It should not be more than 1.

Proprietary Ratio: A variant of debt: equity ratio, it is the ratio of Shareholder's Funds to Total Tangible Assets. The higher the ratio, the stronger is the financial position of the company indicating better capability of bearing financial stress. A smaller ratio is indicative of lesser owned funds and more dependency on borrowed funds.

(iii) Profitability Ratios

Profitability of a company is indicative of efficiency of business operations. The following are important profitability indicators:

EBITDA: Earnings Before Interest, Taxes, Depreciation and Amortization (EBITDA) is an indicator of a company's financial performance. It measures a company's financial performance by computing earnings from core business operations, without including the effects of capital structure, tax rates and depreciation policies.

Net Income: Net income is what remains after subtracting all the costs (namely, business, depreciation, interest, and taxes) from a company's revenues. Net income is sometimes called the bottom line or earnings or net profit.

Earnings per Share: Earnings per share (EPS) serves as an indicator of a company's profitability. It is calculated as Net Income divided by outstanding shares. It is generally considered to be the single most important variable in determining a share's price. It is expressed as Net Profit after tax and dividend on preferred shares divided by number of equity shares.

Dividend per Share: Dividend per share (DPS) is the total dividends paid out over an entire year (including interim dividends) divided by the number of outstanding ordinary shares issued. Dividend is the distribution of a portion of a company's earnings to its shareholders.

The following are the main profitability ratios:

Price: Earnings Ratio (PER): Price-to-earnings ratio is defined as market price per share divided by annual earnings per share. It is the most important equity valuation parameter. There are two versions of PER; Trailing and Forward. Trailing PER uses net income for the most recent 12 month period, divided by the number of common shares outstanding. This is the most common meaning of PER if no other qualifier is specified. Previous four quarterly earnings reports are used and earnings per share are updated quarterly. Forward PER uses estimated net earnings over next 12 months. Estimates are typically derived as the mean of those published by a select group of analysts. Generally a high PER ratio means that investors are anticipating higher growth in the future. The average market is 20-25 times earnings. It varies from industry to industry; a high growth industry has a high PER whereas a utility industry has a low PER.

Price: Earnings Growth Ratio (PEG ratio): PEG ratio is a widely employed indicator of a stock's possible true value. It is defined as PER divided by annual EPS growth rate over a specified time period. Some analysts use 5 year time period whereas others use 1 year time period. Similar to PE ratios, a lower PEG means that the stock is undervalued. The PEG ratio of 1 indicates that a stock is reasonably valued given the expected growth. A lower ratio is considered better and a higher ratio worse.

Price/Book Value (PBR): It is the ratio of the market price of its stock to the book value of the company. Book value per share is the difference between total assets and total liabilities divided by number of outstanding common shares.

Gross Profit Margin: It is the profit a company makes on its cost of sales, or cost of goods sold. It is indicative of how efficiently management uses labor and supplies in the production process. It is expressed as Gross Profit (Sales minus Cost of goods sold) divided by Sales. It varies from industry to industry; the airline industry has a gross margin of about 5%, while the software industry has a gross margin of about 90%.

Operating Profit Margin*: It is the ratio of Earnings Before Interest and Taxes (EBIT) to Sales. This ratio is a measure of the operating leverage a company can achieve in the conduct of the operational part of its business and is indicative of success of the company's management in generating income from the operation of the business.

Net Profit Margin*: It is the ratio of Net Profits after Taxes to Sales.

Overall Profitability Ratio: Also called Return on Investment (ROI) or Return on Capital Employed (ROCE) is the percent return on total capital employed in the business. It is expressed as Operating profit/ Capital employed *100.

Price/Sales Ratio*: Price to sales is calculated by dividing a stock's current price by its revenue per share for the trailing 12 months. It can vary substantially across industries; therefore, it is used to compare similar companies.

Return on Equity (ROE): Also known as Return on Net Worth (RONW) is the ratio of Net Income for the fiscal year to Shareholder's Equity.

Return on Assets (ROA): Also referred to as Return on Investment (ROI), it is calculated by dividing a company's annual earnings by its total assets, expressed as a percentage. ROA gives an idea as to how efficient management is in using its assets to generate earnings.

*(iv) **Activity Ratios***

These ratios indicate the efficiencies of a company in the utilization of available funds, particularly of short term nature.   The following ratios fall in this category: *Inventory Turnover Ratio, Debtors Turnover Ratio, Creditors Turnover Ratio, Fixed Assets Turnover Ratio.*

1.6 Technical Analysis

Technical Analysis is the forecasting of future financial price movements based on an examination of past price movements. The basis of technical analysis is Dow's Theory whose three tenets are: (i) Price discounts everything, (ii) Price movements are not totally random; they follow trends and (iii) "What" Is more important than "Why". It uses only market information - the stock's (or index's) price, its volatility, trading volumes, money flows, long/short ratios etc. The investor buys stock, not the company. He or she considers fundamental analysis, which deals with study balance sheet, profit and loss statement and company's results, a waste of time because all the available information is already incorporated in the stock's price or market sentiment indicators. Technical analysts use price - volume charts of stocks to study the past behaviour of the price and its future prediction. Charting is concerned only with the stock's price relative to its past price and relative to the behaviour of similar stocks. Technical analysts try to detect trends and shifts in those trends. It is used to make buy/sell decisions, not to determine any 'true value' of the company or its stock. It deals in relative prices, not absolute values. It is extensively used in trading. This method does not require the knowledge of financial statements or finance or the economy. Technical Analysis has however certain limitations. The technical indicators give possible entry and exit points; the forecasting accuracy is not 100%. Though Technical Analysis is mostly used for short term trading, it can be successfully employed for timing the long term buy and sell decisions by using longer term time frame charts like weekly and monthly. Charting and basics of Technical Analysis have been described in chapter 2.

1.7 Combining Fundamental and Technical Analysis

The two techniques of fundamental and technical analysis are often opposite of each other but these can be combined together to the advantage of investor. Fundamental analysis attempts to determine the value of a share by analysing a company's financials from its annual report and using qualitative data about the environment in which it operates. This value is often called intrinsic value. The simplest form of fundamental analysis is by using fundamental ratios such as the price to earnings ratio, price to book value or the dividend yield. Technical analysis offers a different view of a stock. It is based on the belief that all that is known about a stock is reflected in its price and volume. The market is made up of a very large number of people who may have very different views on the market, making both long and short term decisions. The activity of these very large numbers of investors and traders results in different patterns emerging in the market. Technical analysts attempt to recognise these patterns and take advantage of them when making their investment decisions. Though Technical Analysis is more favoured for trading but investors can use it gainfully with longer time frame charts like weekly or monthly. In nut shell these two techniques can be gainfully employed to:

Fundamental Analysis	1.Select stocks with sound financials and future growth potential
	2.Dtermine whether a stock is under- or overvalued relative to its intrinsic value
	3.Avoid overvalued stocks or high debt companies to lessen risk
Technical Analysis	1.Time to buy the selected fundamentally sound stock(s)
	2. Exit when the stock goes sour or under performs

1.8 Risk

Before proceeding further it is necessary to study risk involved in investing in shares. Broadly speaking there are three types of risks in the investment in stocks: (1) market risk, (2) industry risk and (3) company risk. Market risk is inherent to the entire market. It is also called systematic risk and cannot be diversified or avoided. It arises from fluctuation of interest rates, recession, money flow across countries, politics and wars. Unsystematic risk, also called industry risk affects a specific industry due to various factors such as business environment, shortage of raw material, high rate of taxation, import and export policy, foreign exchange rate etc. It can be mitigated by diversification, that is, by investing across several industries. Company risk is specific to a company and may arise from credit or default risk, sudden strike in the company, poor management etc. It can be offset by proper diversification or by investing in two or companies of the same sector/ industry. Unsystematic risk can be minimised by investing across sectors/ industries. Too much of diversification does not pay; it loses the basic objective and increases the overhead of monitoring portfolio on regular basis. As a rule of thumb one should invest across at least 6 sectors and buy stocks of 2-3 top companies in each sector. The total number of shares in a portfolio should normally not exceed 20. Research says that holding more than 20 shares in a portfolio does not add to the benefit of diversification but increases the monitoring overhead.

Return from stock is directly related to risk, that is, higher the risk, higher the return. As risk tolerance capacity of individuals is limited and varies with earnings and age of investors, risk/ return tradeoff is a must before stepping into stock market. As stock markets are, to some extent, are risky, all trades or investments in stock market must be in favour of a better risk reward ratio suited to the risk tolerance capacity of the investor.

The following pyramid is indicative of ideal investments across various asset classes:

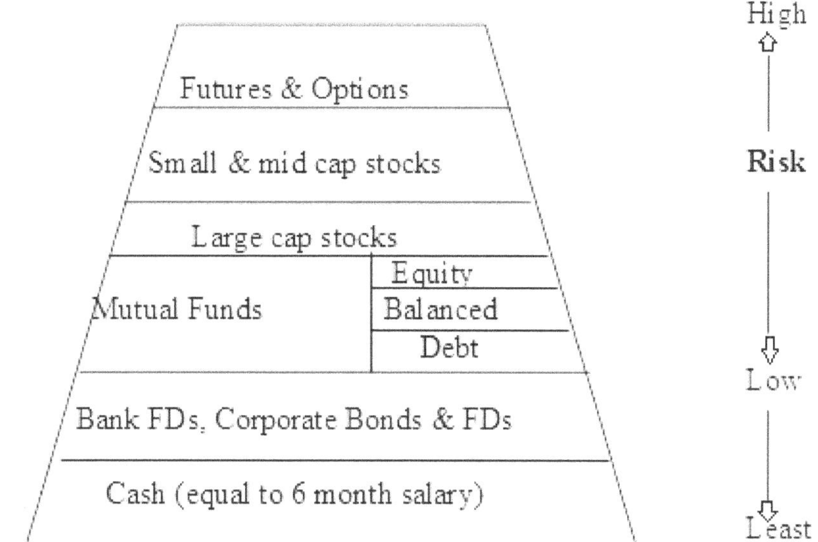

Fig 1.1: Ideal Asset Allocation Pyramid

----------OOOOOOO-----------

Chapter 2

CHARTING

"If you have trouble imagining a 20% loss in the stock market, you should't be in the stock." – *John Bogle*

2.1 Introduction

Charts of shares are visual clue as to what is cooking in the market or in a particular share. The study of charts is called Technical Analysis, which It is radically different from fundamental analysis. Fundamental analysis is a kind of post mortem i.e. it analyses the stock price after disclosure of the company results when the share price corrects to its true value whereas technical analysts can forecast the share price much in advance, sometimes even up to six months before. Technical analysts, just like medical doctors, who read X-rays, study charts of share prices and predict future price. They believe that the market price of a share is determined by the interaction of supply and demand forces. Supply and demand are, in turn, influenced by a variety of factors, both fundamental and behavioral. Technical analysis is much easier than fundamental analysis and is gaining popularity. It is more suited to short term trades. It is widely used among traders and financial professionals, and is very often used by active day traders. Here long term chart patterns will be described that will help you in identifying long term trends and entry and exit opportunities.

The stock price moves in the following four stages:

Stage1- Accumulation: Stage 1 is the horizontal trading range that begins the method. After declining out of stage 4, price moves sideways, sometimes rising above the 30-week moving average and sometimes not. The moving average flattens out, following price horizontally. Price is choppy but usually forming a sideways price movement.

Stage 2- Mark-up or Uphill Run: In this sage price breaks out of the trading range of stage 1 on impressive volume. The moving average turns up. Price makes higher highs and higher lows. Price remains above the moving average. Beginning of this stage is the ideal time to buy.

Stage 3- Distribution: Stage 3 is the top. Price levels out and begins to move horizontally again. The moving average is climbing but flattens out, eventually catching price, slicing through it. Volume may increase as price remains sideways. According to some experts the traders should take profits in this stage, but investors can hold on by selling half their position. If price moves up, forming another stage 2 advance, then continue to hold. A downward breakout from the trading range should signal a sale.

Stage 4- Downhill run or panic selling: Stage 4 is the downhill run due to panic selling. Price breaks out downward from the stage 3 top and may pull back into the trading range. After that, though, price continues to fall down. The moving average (average of past n days prices) usually remains above the stock as price drops. The following chart of Orchid Chemicals from 2009 to April 2013 (Fig.1) shows these stages.

Fig. 1- Weekly chart of Orchid Pharma showing four stages of stock price movement [Chart plotted in Metrastock]

In nut shell technical analysis is the study of charts of stock prices. Share prices of thousands of shares listed on Bombay Stock Exchange (BSE) and National Stock Exchange (NSE) are available on their websites www.bseindia.com and www.nseindia.com respectively. Their intraday and historical charts are available at www.bseindia.com. Many other free sites, such as, www.finance.yahoo.co,in, www.google.com/finance, www.moneycontrol.com, www.livemint.com, www.icharts.in, www.daytradingshares.com, www.business-standard.com, www.in.investing.com, www.ETmarkets.com etc. and of course all paid sites provide charts of shares of listed companies. You can even perform a lot of analysis with free charts.

2.1 Charts

Prices in a chart can be displayed in three styles: bar, line, and candlestick.

Bar: A vertical bar displays high, low, opening and closing price in a given unit of time, e.g. daily in end-of-day chart and 1 or 5 minute interval in an intraday chart. Opening and closing prices are displayed by small horizontal bar on the right and left of the vertical bar as shown in the figure 2(a).

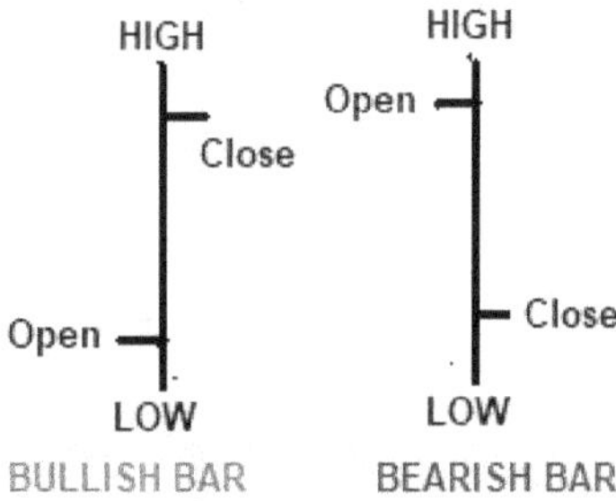

Fig. 2(a) Bullish and Beraish bars

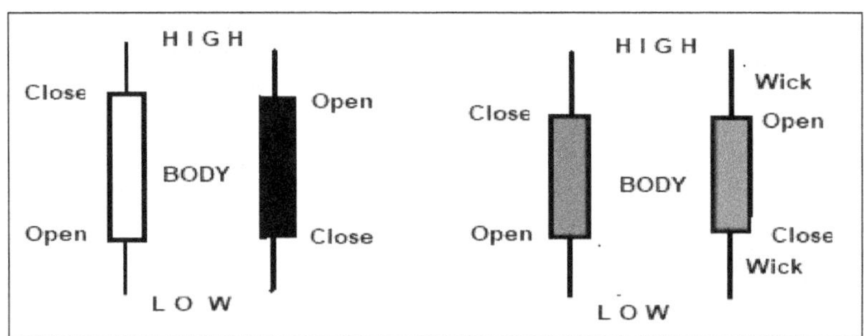

Fig..2(b) : Bullish and Bearish candles

Candlestick: It is similar to bar except that opening and closing prices are represented by a thick hollow white or green) candle or solid (black or red) candle, called body of the candlestick (Fig.2(b)). The thin vertical lines projecting outside the candle represent low and high prices and are called shadows of the candle. A candlestick is black (bearish) if the closing price is lower than the opening price. A candlestick is white (bullish) if the closing price is higher than the opening price. Green or white (hollow) candles are called bullish (rising price) candles and red or black candles bearish (falling price).

Line: A line chart simply connects the closing prices from one period to the next. This type of chart is ideal for securities with no high or low price data (i.e. mutual funds).

Fig. 2(c) shows typical daily bar, candlestick (or just candle) and line charts of three different stocks on the common horizontal (time) axis. Vertical axis shows price. Each bar or candle represents daily price fluctuations. Charts can also be plotted with 1,2,5,10,30 minute, 1 hour, weekly, monthly intervals or quarterly and yearly intervals. The 1,2,5,10,30- minute charts are suitable for day trading whereas daily, weekly and monthly charts are well suited to medium (a few months) and long term (more than 1 year) analysis. Quarterly and yearly charts are used by institutional investors. Daily charts can normally cover upto 3 year data whereas weekly and monthly charts can cover much longer data upto 10 years or more.

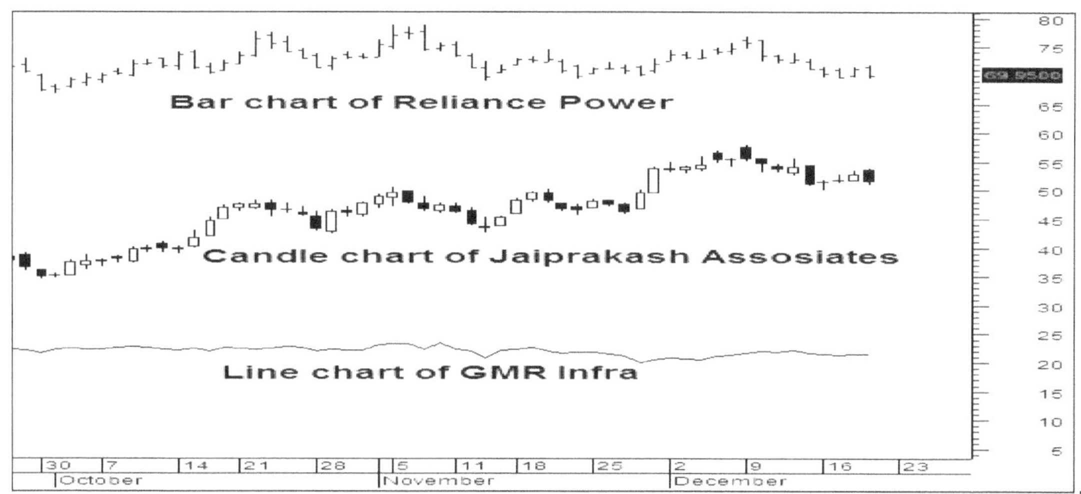

Fig 2(c): Typical daily bar, candle and line charts

2.3 Chart Patterns

Charts often exhibit break out and break down patterns where one can enter and exit the stock. The following are some important patterns:

(a) Trend

The trend is the observable direction of the market -- up, down, or sideways. In fact, during a strong bull market over 90% of stocks can be trending upward together. The trend can be analyzed in three timeframes - short-term (days to weeks), intermediate-term (weeks to months), or long-term (months to years). The chart of ICICI Bank (see figure below) shows all these trends. The long-term trend is the most dominating. There is an old saying that "Trend is your friend". One of the keys to successful investing is to follow trend, that is, buy when the upward trend begins, and continue riding upward journey so long is trend is up and sell when the trend becomes flat or reverses. Investors should observe long term trends (weekly) whereas traders follow short term trends (daily, hourly or 5 minutes).

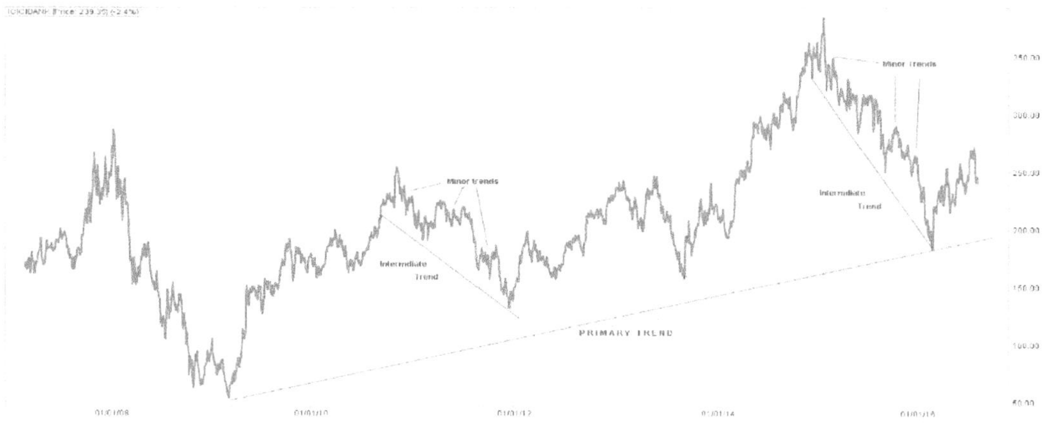

Fig. Weekly chart of ICICI Bank showing Primary, Intermediate and Short term Trends

In a rising trend the stock prices make higher tops and higher bottoms. Likewise lower tops and lower bottoms will be made in a down trend. By drawing trend lines one can see the distinct trend. The following weekly chart of Nifty 50 (see Fig. below) from 2007 to 2010 depicts down trend, flat (sideways) trend and uptrend marked by trend lines.

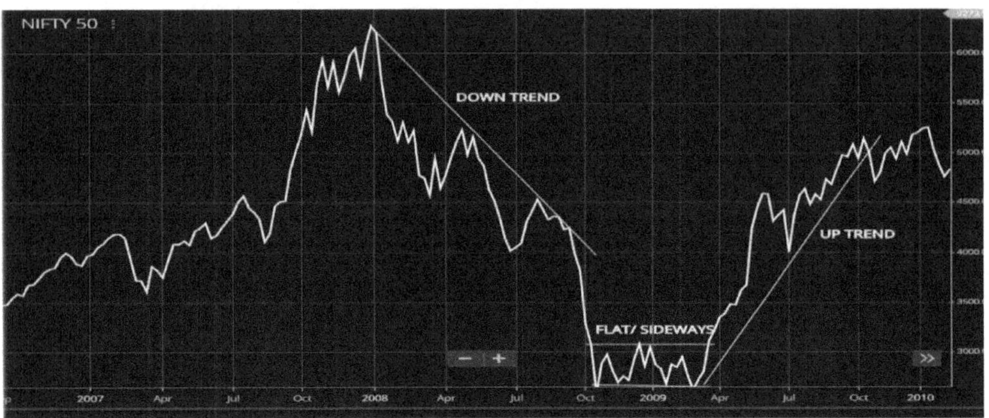

Fig. - Weekly Chart of Nifty from 2007 to 2010 showing down, flat and up trends

(b) Trend lines A trend line is a straight line that connects two or more top or bottom points. In future it can act as a support or resistance line or both. More the number of points it touches, stronger the trend is. A valid trend line has at least three points touching it. More the number of points it touches, the greater is the reliability of the trend line. Length (time period) also determines its reliability, the longer the trend line, more reliable it is. High volumes confirm the trend. In an ideal trend line the points should be well spaced; these should neither too near nor too far. In an ideal trend line the lows or highs, it touches, should be evenly spaced. If the lows or highs are too close, the reaction highs or lows (pull-ups and pull-backs) may not be clearly seen. Similarly if the lows or highs are far apart, the trend line may become shaky. In such cases you need to redraw your trend line to rectify the above situation. The weekly chart of Sensex (see Fig. below) shows a near ideal trend line. The points on the trend line are nearly evenly spaced. Observe the up move for a long period of 3 years indicates a bull phase. This trend line is pierced by Sensex curve on 24 February 2020. Soon after Sensex fell below 200 WMA (Weekly Moving Average).

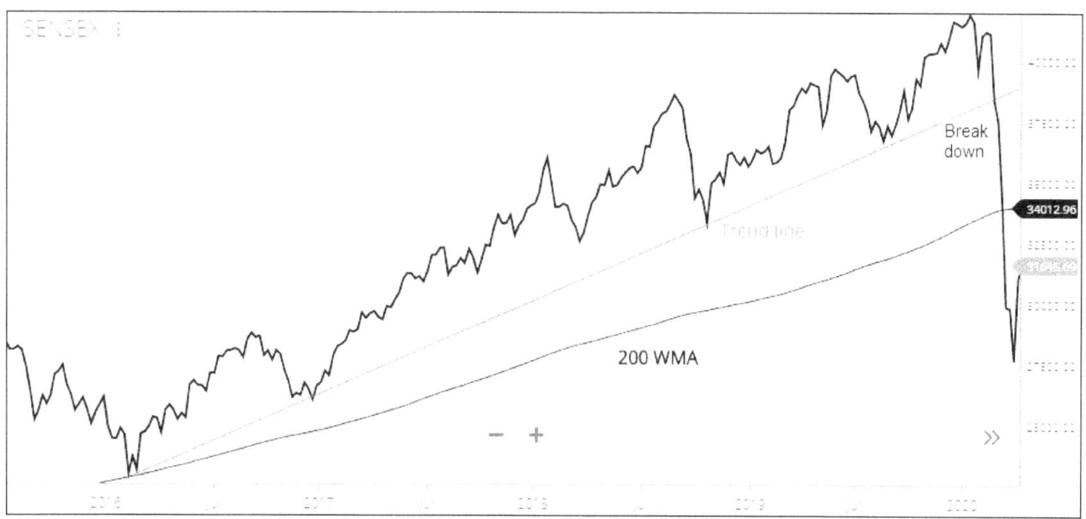

Fig - Weekly chart of Sensex showing Trend Line [chart created in Zerodha.com]

The steepness of the trend line has serious implications. Too steep a trend line cannot persist for long. It indicates sharp moves in the price for a brief period. Such trend lines cannot offer meaningful support or resistance.   Volume also serves as powerful indicator for upward or downward break out. Violation of up trend line with high volumes means new upward trend. Similarly piercing of down trend line with high volume will signal end of up move and a new downward journey.

(c) Support and Resistance Lines

The concept of support and resistance is quite basic, yet powerful enough to point out upward and downward breakouts. When the stock prices are rising, there is a resistance level which halts its upward movement due to sufficient selling pressure. This level meets supply pressure as number of points touched by the stock price. This line is broken by a strong up move supported by a large volume, that is, when buyers overpower the sellers. Conversely, support level is the level at which the fall of share prices is arrested due to sufficient buying. The share is bought at this level by those investors or traders who see enough value in the share. This level is broken due to heavy selling pressure when the sellers overpower the buyers. The daily chart of Nifty (see Fig. below) shows Resistance and Support lines. Breach of these lines (AB and GF) signals trend reversal.

Fig - Resistance and Support lines the daily chart of Nifty

Stock prices often move in three basic channels (i) Up, (ii) Down and (iii) Sideways channels. Fig. below shows the horizontal and upward channels in weekly chart of Yes Bank.

Fig.– Horizontal and upward channels in weekly chart of Yes Bank

(d)Triangles

Triangles are formed during the sideways movements and can be seen on the charts by drawing upper and lower trend lines. The upper trend connects the tops and lower trend line connects bottom points. There are three types of triangle formations such as symmetrical, ascending and descending triangles. Ascending triangles are generally bullish whereas descending triangles are generally bearish. Symmetrical triangles are neutral. Ascending and descending triangle patterns are very popular.

Ascending continuation triangle: An Ascending Continuation Triangle is considered a bullish signal. It indicates a possible   continuation of the current uptrend. It comprises two converging trend lines, the lower trend line which is rising while the upper trend line is horizontal (see figure below). This pattern is confirmed when the price breaks out of the triangle formation to close above the upper trend line. Volume is an important factor to consider Typically, volume follows a reliable pattern: volume should diminish as the price swings back and forth between an increasingly narrow

range of highs and lows. However, when breakout occurs, there should be a noticeable increase in volume. If this volume picture is not clear, the investor should be cautious about decision based on this triangle. The triangle is a relatively short-term pattern. It may take one to three months to form. When prices are close to or touch the 200 day Moving Average this signal is considered stronger.

Descending Continuation Triangle: A Descending Continuation Triangle is considered a bearish signal, indicating that the current down trend may continue. It features two converging trend lines. The bottom trend line is horizontal and the top trend line slopes downward (see figure). This pattern is confirmed when the price breaks out of the triangle formation to close below the lower trend line. Volume is an important factor to consider. Typically, volume follows a reliable pattern: volume should   diminish as the price swings back and forth   between an increasingly narrow range of highs and lows.

However, when breakout occurs, there should be a noticeable increase in volume. The triangle is a relatively short-term pattern. It may take from one to three months to form. When prices are close to or touch the 200 day moving average this signal is considered stronger.

Symmetrical Continuation Triangle (Bullish): A bullish symmetrical continuation triangle indicates that the current uptrend may continue. It comprises two trend lines, the lower one ascending and the upper one descending (see figure below). This pattern is confirmed when the price breaks out of the triangle formation to close above the upper trend line. The volume is a reliable indicator: it should diminish with the progression of the triangle with a noticeable increase at the breakout. The closer the breakout occurs to the apex the less reliable the formation. As a general rule prices should break out the upper trend line - somewhere between three-quarters and two-thirds of the horizontal width of the formation. The duration of the pattern is an indicator of the duration of the influence of this pattern, the longer the pattern the longer it will take for the price to reach its target.

Symmetrical Continuation Triangle (Bearish): A bearish symmetrical continuation triangle indicates that the current downtrend may continue. It comprises two converging trend lines, the lower ascending and the upper descending.(see figure below). This pattern is confirmed when the price breaks out of the triangle formation below the lower trend line. However, when the breakout occurs, there should be a noticeable increase in volume. Further the break out should occur well before the pattern reaches the apex of the triangle, the farther the breakout occurs to the apex the more reliable the formation.

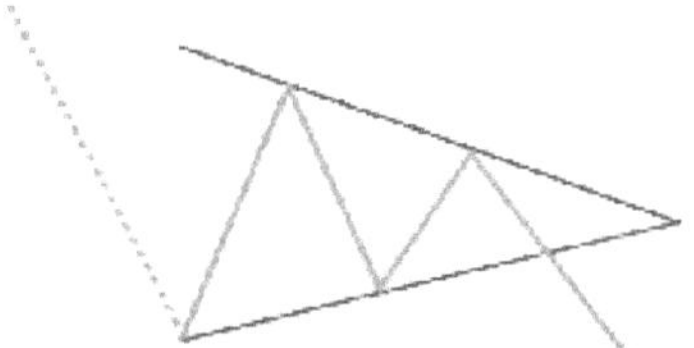

(e) Head and Shoulders

A Head and Shoulders pattern is considered a bearish signal. It indicates a possible reversal of the

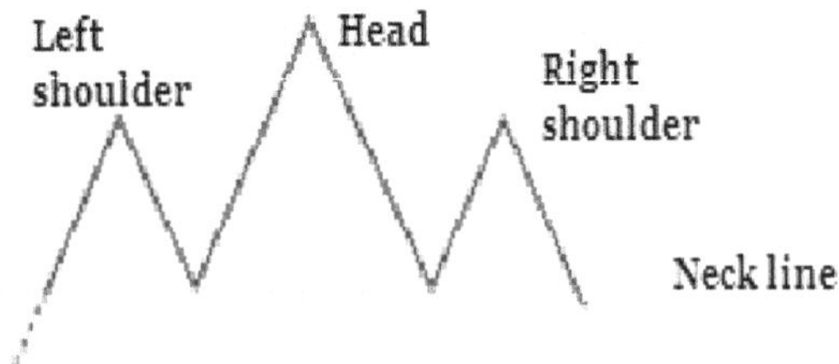

current uptrend to a new down trend. It is one of the most reliable of all formations and is very popular pattern among investors. The classic Head and Shoulders looks like a human head with shoulders on either side of the head. A perfect example of the pattern has three sharp high points, created by three successive rallies in the price of the stock (see figure}.The first point - the left shoulder - occurs as the price of the stock in a rising market hits a high and then falls back. The second point - the head - happens when prices rise to new high (higher than the left shoulder) and then fall back again. The third point - the right shoulder - occurs when prices rise again but don't hit the high of the head. Prices then fall back once again. The shoulders are lower than the head and, in a classic formation, are often roughly equal to one another. A key element of the pattern is the neckline. The neckline is formed by drawing a line connecting two low price points of the formation. The first low point occurs at the end of the left shoulder and the beginning of the uptrend to the head. The second shoulder marks the end of the head and the beginning of the upturn to the right shoulder. The neckline can be horizontal or it can slope up or down. The pattern is complete when the support provided by the neckline is broken and the price moves below the neckline. The pattern is not confirmed until the price closes below the neckline. Volume is also a very important factor in the formation of a valid Head and Shoulder pattern. It is highest at the beginning of left shoulder and lowest on the right shoulder. Low volume levels on the right shoulder are a strong sign of a reversal. Volume often increases when the neckline is broken as the reversal is now complete and downside pressure begins in the earnest that is, very high volumes are seen on the downward breakout. The size of both the shoulders should be approximately equal but there may be many variations such as varying width and height of shoulders, drooping shoulders, flat and multiple shoulders etc. The pattern normally takes three months time in its formation and may last up to six months. The Head and Shoulders pattern should be above 50 day Moving Average for short duration patterns and 200 day Moving Average for longer patterns.

In the above chart of the neckline is slanting downwards. It many cases it may be horizontal or slanting upwards. The following chart of State Bank of India shows an upward neckline. This is a long term pattern made in about eight months. The neck line is well above 200 DMA.

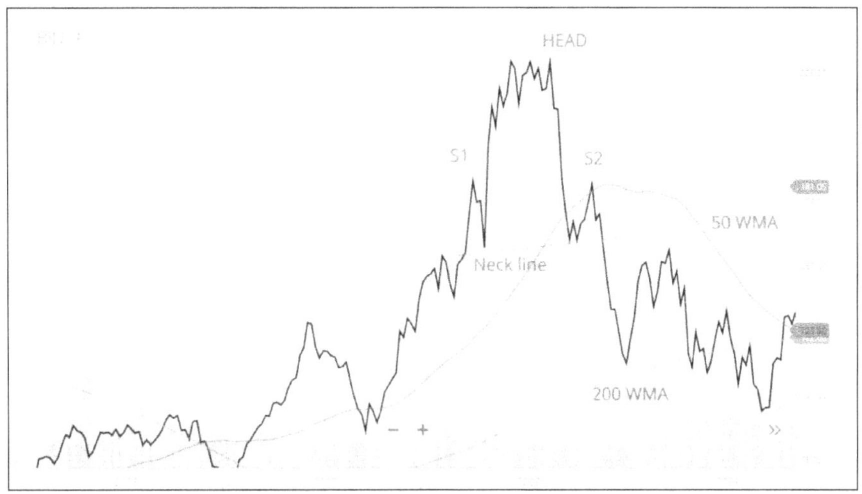

Fig. Weekly chart of State Bank of India showing Head and Shoulders pattern [chart created in Zerodha.com]

(f) Inverted Head and Shoulder

An inverted head and shoulder is considered a bullish signal. It indicates a possible reversal of the current downtrend into a new uptrend. It is formed following a major downtrend in the stock. Volume is crucial to this pattern. There is an increasing volume at the breakout. An ideal inverted head and shoulder has three sharp low points created by three successive reactions in the price of the stock (see figure below). The first point - the left shoulder – occurs as the price of the stock in a falling market hits a new low and then rises in a minor recovery. The second point - the head happens when prices fall from the high of the left shoulder to an even lower level and then rise again. The third point - the right shoulder - occurs when prices fall again but don't hit the low of the head. Prices then rise again once they have hit the low of the right shoulder. The lows of the shoulders are higher than that of the head and are often roughly equal to one another. The neckline is formed by drawing a line connecting the two high price points of the formation. The neckline usually points down in this pattern. The pattern is complete only if the stock price closes above the neckline.

As an example of Inverted Head and Shoulder look at the chart of Auropharma (Fig. below). Note the massive breakout from neck line. Further the rise above the neckline is equal to the fall below the neck line, which is the ideal case. The formation is well below 200 DMA line.

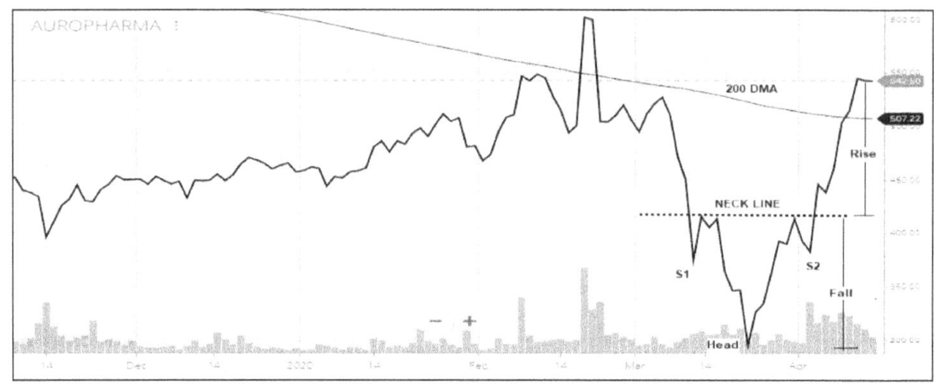

Fig. Daily chart of Auropharma showing Inverted Head and Shoulder [chart drawn in Zerodha.com]

(g) Double Bottom Pattern

A Double Bottom is considered a bullish signal, indicating a possible reversal of the current downtrend to a new uptrend. It marks a downtrend in the process of becoming an uptrend. It is among the most common patterns. A double bottom occurs when prices form two distinct lows on a chart (see figure below). It is complete only when price rises above the high end of the second low. Some conditions should be fulfilled in the formation of a double bottom. After the first bottom is formed, a rise of at least 10% should follow the formation of first bottom. The second bottom returning back to the previous low (plus or minus 3%) should have a lower volume than the first. Volume increases again when the pattern completes, breaking through the confirmation point. Some analysts maintain that the rise between the two bottoms should be at least 20% and the lows should be spaced at least a month apart. It ranges from a few weeks in case of daily charts to one year in case of weekly charts. If the double bottom is above the moving average then this pattern should be considered less reliable. For short duration patterns 50 day Moving Average and for longer patterns 200 day Moving Average should be used.

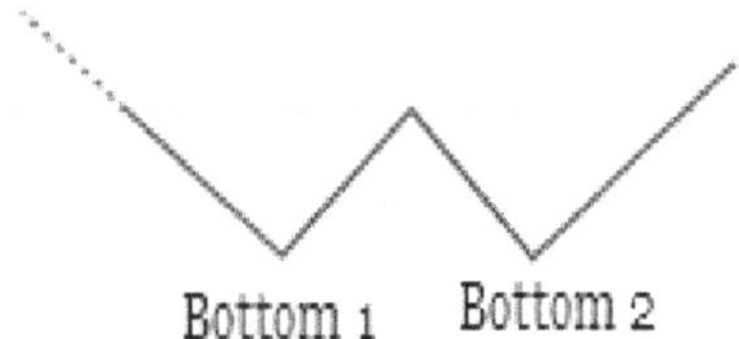

(h) Double Top Pattern

 A Double Top is considered a bearish signal, indicating a possible reversal of the current uptrend to a new downtrend. It marks an uptrend in the process of becoming a downtrend. Also called an "M" formation because of the pattern it creates on the chart, it is one of the most frequently seen and common pattern. It consists of two well-defined sharp peaks at approximately the same price level. The two tops are distinct and sharp (see figure below). The pattern is complete when prices decline below the lowest low in the formation see figure below). Some conditions apply to an effective double chart pattern. After the first top is formed, a reaction of at least 10% should follow. The second high (plus or minus 3%) should have lower volume than the first. Some analysts hold the view that the decline between the two tops should be at least 20% and the peaks should be spaced at least a month apart. It ranges from a few weeks in case of daily charts to one year in case weekly charts. Generally, the longer the time between the two tops, the more important the pattern is as a good reversal signal. It is not unusual for a few months to a year to pass between the dates of the two tops. Volume tends to be heaviest during the first peak, lighter on the second and high again at the time of breakout. The double top should be above the moving average. For short duration patterns 50 day Moving Average and for longer duration patterns 200 day Moving Average should be used. Further the deeper the trough between the two tops, more reliable is the pattern.

(i)Broadening Formation

Broadening pattern is formed the prices make increasing large up and down swings, that is, the prices move within diverging trend lines. The prices tend to behave in an abrupt manner with wild swings. The smart money is out from the market. The volume is also erratic during this pattern. This is generally seen at the end of a prolonged uptrend and signals reversal of the current trend.

(j) Flags (Bullish)

A Flag (Bullish) follows a steep or nearly vertical rise in price, and consists of two parallel trend lines that form a rectangular flag shape. The flag can be horizontal or slightly downtrend. (see figure below). It is considered a bullish signal, indicating that the current uptrend may continue. The pattern is confirmed when the price crosses the upper trend line of the flag and continues the original upward price movement.   The sharp price   increase is   sometimes referred to as the "flagpole" or "mast". The pattern is confirmed when the price crosses the upper trend line of the flag. The volume is high initially but diminishes gradually. The formation takes 5 days to 2-3 weeks to complete.

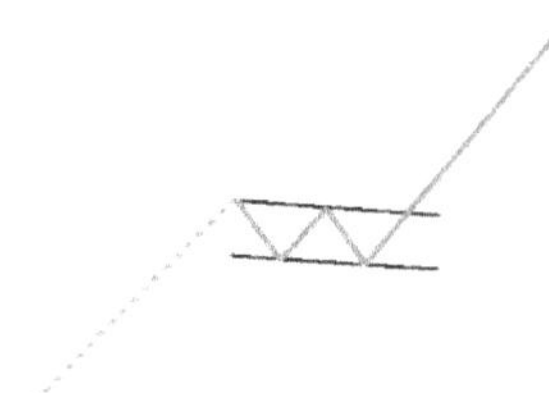

The following chart of Indoco Remedies shows a flag formation. Note the short duration and diminished volume during the flag formation.

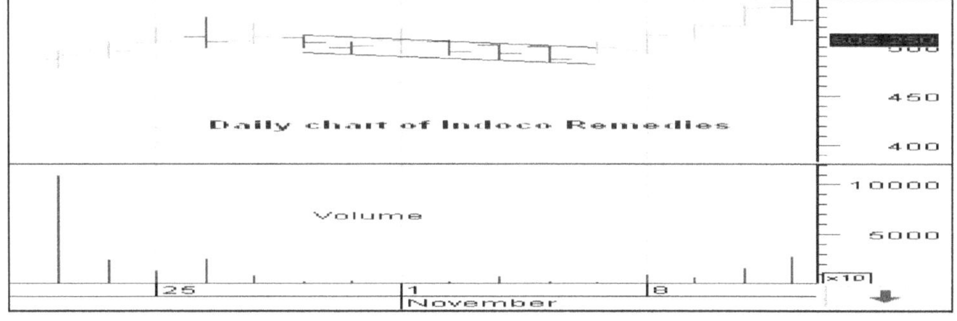

Fig - Daily chart of Indoco Remedies showing Flag formation

(k) Pennant (Bullish)

A Pennant (Bullish) follows a steep or nearly vertical rise in price, and consists of two converging trend lines that form a narrow, tapering flag shape (see figure below). It is similar in shape to Symmetrical Triangle or Wedge flag but shorter in duration and horizontal in direction. Initially volume is high but tends to decrease as the pennant develops.

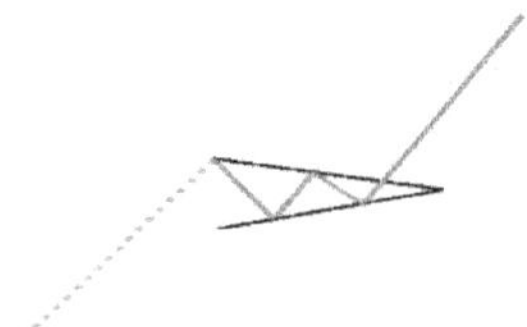

The following chart of Punjab Woolcombers shows a Pennant formation:

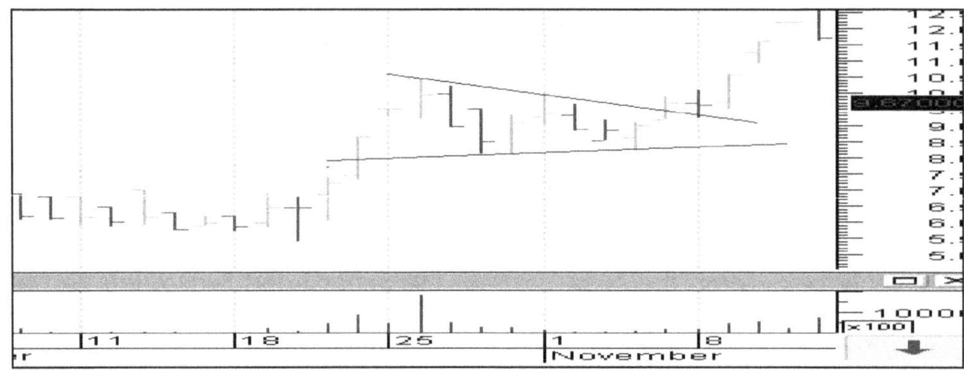

Fig - Daily chart of Punjab Woolcombers showing Pennant formation.

(l) Wedge (Bullish)

A Wedge (Bullish) is considered a bullish signal. It indicates a possible continuation of the current uptrend. It consists of two converging trend lines slanting downward (see figure below). A bullish signal occurs when prices break above the upper trend line. This pattern is formed over the weeks or months. The trend appears to be downward but the long- term range is still upward.   The duration of the pattern is considered to be an indicator of the duration of the influence of this pattern. The longer the pattern the longer it will take for the price to move to the Target. The shorter the pattern the sooner the price move. Its volume diminishes as the pattern progresses to form.

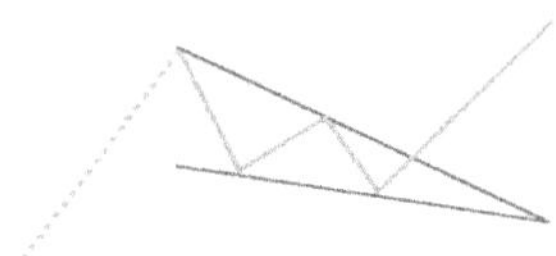

(m) Rounded Top

Rounded Bottom is an elongated and U-shaped, and is sometimes referred to as rounding turns, bowls or saucers.(see figure below). The pattern is confirmed when the price breaks out above its moving average. It is considered a bullish signal, indicating a possible reversal of the current downtrend to a new uptrend. The price pattern forms a gradual bowl shape. Volume tends to decrease as bearishness wanes and investors   become   indecisive. Following a period of relative inactivity, at the bottom of the bowl, the price pattern starts its upward turn.   Rounded   bottom is long-term pattern. The pattern can occur over a period of about 3 weeks, but can also be observed over several years.

The following weekly chart of JK Paper shows a Rounded Bottom formation. Note the diminishing volume in the middle of the pattern and increased volume at the end of the pattern. This pattern lasts for 6 years signaling a huge upward breakout at point B.

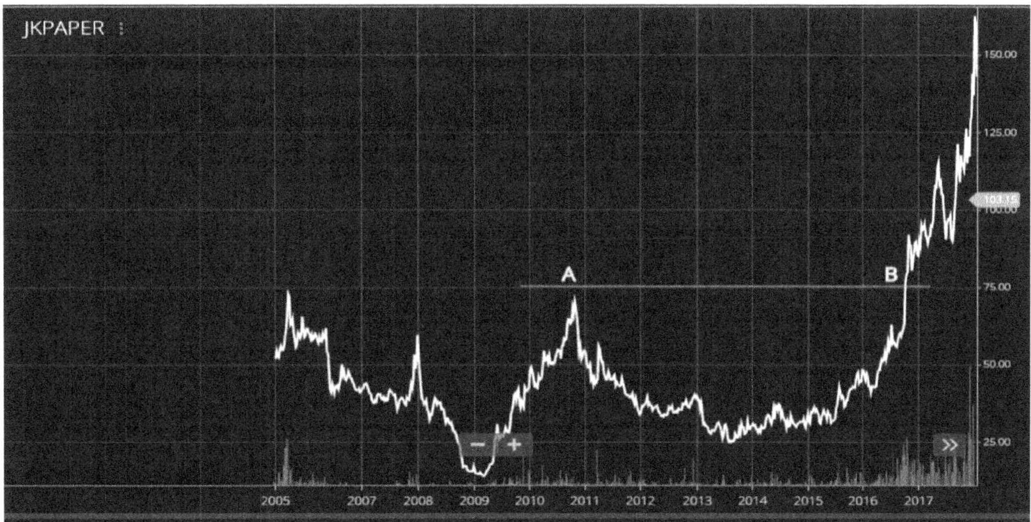

Fig - Daily chart of Astrazeneca Phama showing Rounded Bottom

(n) Cup and Handle

It is a bullish continuation pattern where the upward trend pauses, trades down, and continues again the upward direction upon the completion of the pattern. It resembles the shape of a cup with handle. This pattern can range from several months to a year.   This pattern is a signal of consolidation within a trend, where the weaker investors leave the security and new buyers and resolute holders stay in the security. Some conditions are necessary for formation of powerful cup and handle pattern. First, prior up trend is a must but the uptrend should be in its initial stage: the larger the prior trend, the lower is the potential for a large breakout after the pattern has been completed. Its shape should be a nicely rounded formation, similar to a semi-circle. The height of the cup should be between one-third and two-thirds the size of the previous upward movement. The handle should be a down move and it can retrace one-third of the up move of the cup. Again, most importantly the breakout should be supported by strong volume: the stronger the volume on the upward breakout, greater is the possibility of strong up move. The following weekly chart of Hindalco shows Cup and Handle formation.

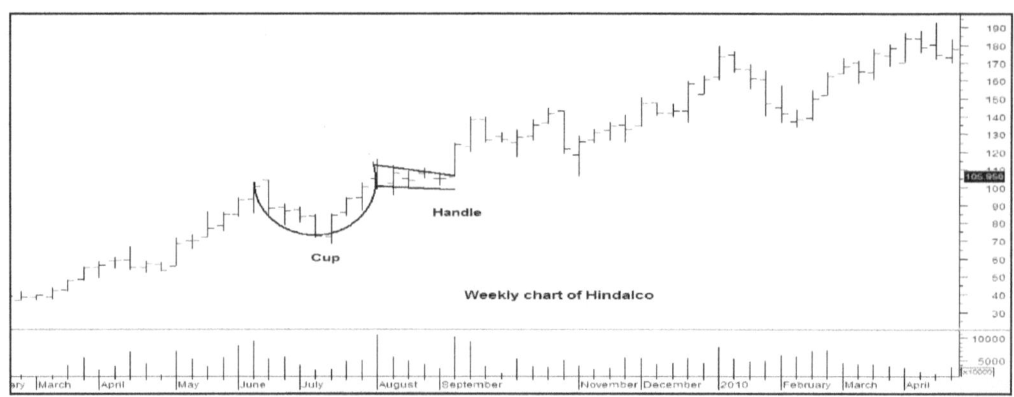

Fig - Weekly chart of Hindalco showing Cup and Handle

(o) Long Base formation

The Long Base pattern is a period of churning and consolidation during which the stock is being accumulated. It is also a period when the stock is out of favor and public interest is very low. You should look for companies that have relatively solid fundamentals that are either in this basing phase or have just broken out. Once the price breaks out of the range, a buy signal is rendered and the growth phase begins. This is probably the most promising and profitable pattern that an investor can identify, and it happens again and again over a wide range of stocks. The following monthly chart of Orchid Chemicals   shows 2 year long base formation from March 2001 to March 2003. Note that traders interest is missing in this period. There is price and volume burst in March 2003.

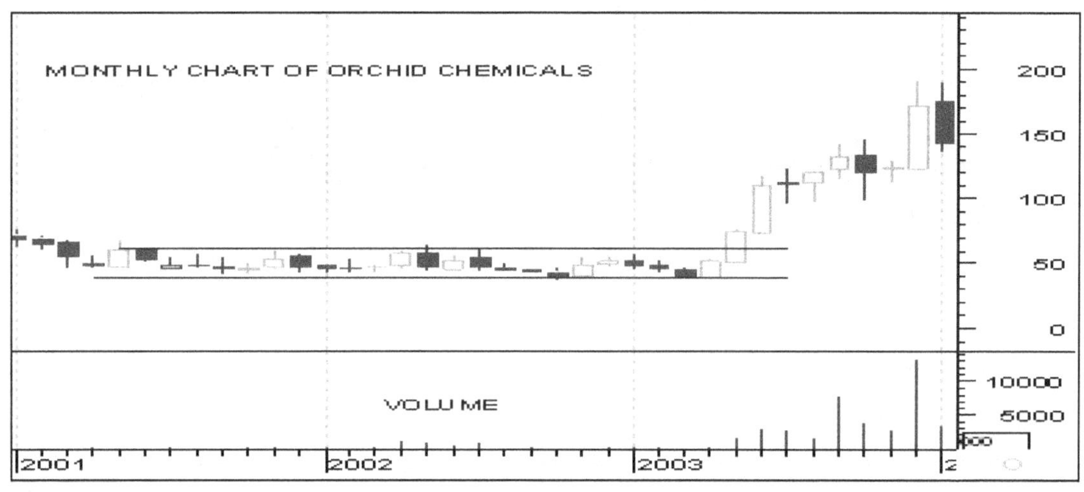

Fig- Monthly chart of Orchid Chemicals showing long base formation.

2.4 Indicators

Indicators, used in technical analysis, provide an extremely useful source of additional information. These help identify momentum, trends, volatility and various other aspects of a security. They are best used in conjunction with price movement, chart patterns and other indicators. There are two main types of indicators: leading and lagging. A leading indicator precedes price movements, predicting the price movement in advance, while a lagging indicator is a confirmation tool because it follows price movement. A leading indicator is thought to be the strongest during periods of sideways or trading ranges, while the lagging indicators are useful during trending periods.

Indicators are based on the price and the volume movements of a security and measure money flow, trends, volatility and momentum etc. Indicators provide additional information to the analysis of securities. These are used in two main ways: to confirm price movement and the quality of chart patterns, and to give buy and sell signals. They may be range bound or non-bounded. The range bound indicators are also called oscillators and are the most common type of indicators. Oscillators have a range, for example between zero and 100. Non-bounded indicators form buy and sell signals along with displaying strength or weakness. The two main ways that indicators are used to form buy and sell signals in technical analysis are through crossovers and divergence. Crossovers are the most popular and are reflected when either the price moves through the moving average, or when two different moving averages cross over each other. The second way indicators are used is through divergence, which happens when the direction of the price trend and the direction of the indicator trend are moving in the opposite direction. This signals that the direction of the price trend is weakening.

(1) Non-range Bound Indicators

The following are main non-range bound indicators:

(a) Average Directional Index: The average directional index (ADX) is a trend indicator that is used to measure the strength of a current trend. The indicator does not define the direction of the current but can identify the momentum of the trend. ADX is a combination of two price movement measures: the positive directional indicator (+DI) and the negative directional indicator (-DI). +DI measures the strength of the upward trend while -DI measures the strength of the downward trend. These two measures are also plotted along with the ADX line. Measured on a scale between zero and 100, readings below 20 signal a weak trend while readings above 40 signal a strong trend. Fig. below shows daily chart of SBI with ADX indicator. On two occasions, 8th October (line XX') and 4th March (line YY') ADX crossed 40 line, which indicated trend reversal with strong momentum.

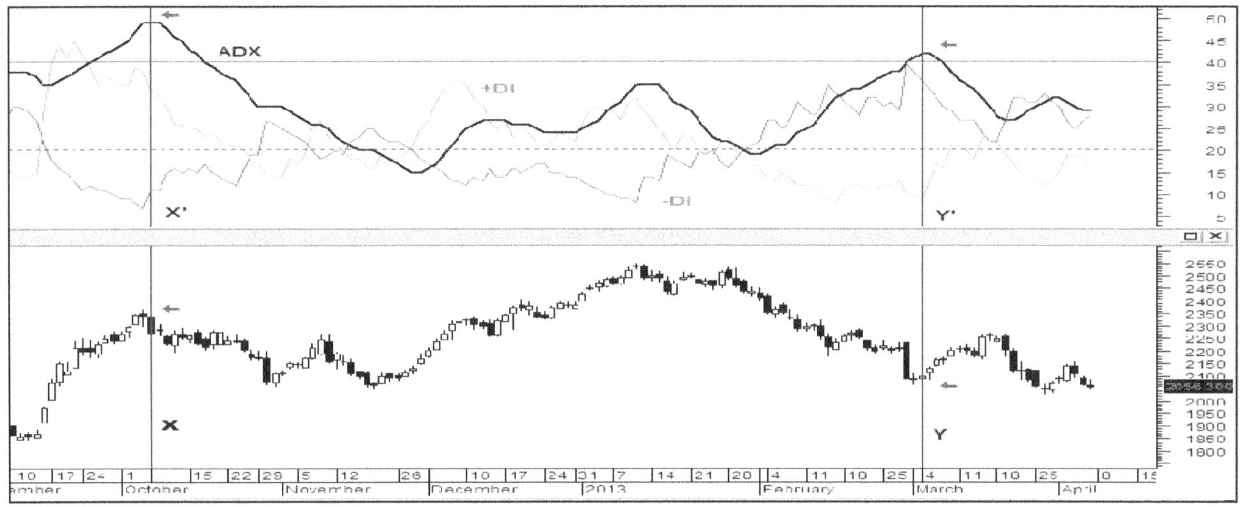

Fig. Daily chart of SBI with ADX indicator [Chart created in Metastock]

ADX can be used to identify buy signal. The following chart of Amar   Remedies illustrates this point:

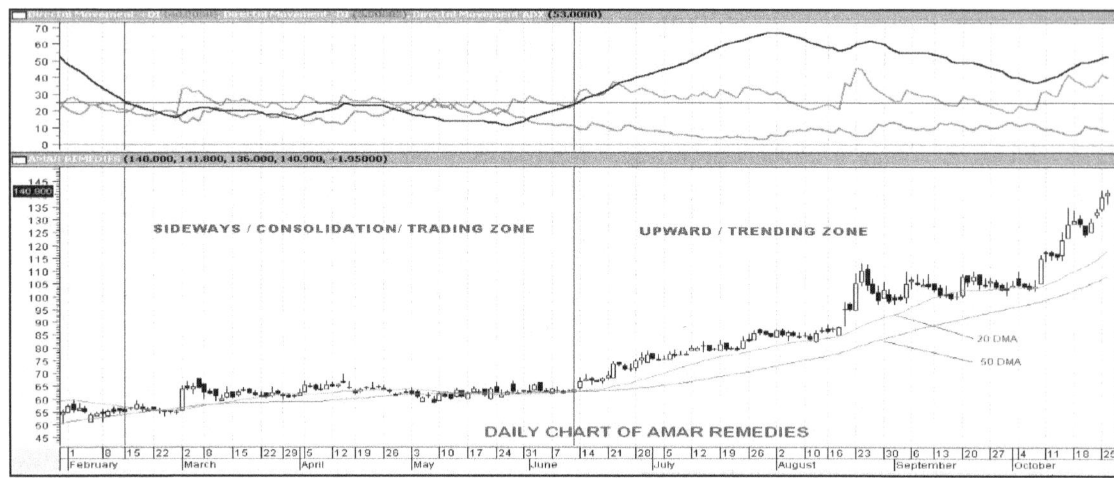

Fig. Daily chart of Amar Remedies showing ADX [chat created in Metastock]

In this chart of Amar Remedies from Feb to Oct 2010, the ADX indicator is shown as thick black line. The green and the red lines are the +DI and –DI. The left hand side area, where ADX is below 25, shows sideways or trading zone and the area on right hand side, where ADX is above 25, marks up move or trending zone. In the trading range ADX is showing a low reading and the stock is chopping around sideways. The rise of ADX from the low of 15 from the left side to above 30 on the right side signals the entry of the stock in the new upward territory. This up move is confirmed by crossover of 20, 50 day moving averages. This is the time to buy the stock.

(b) Moving Average

It is the average of past n-periods or sum of prices of last n-days divided by for example an 8 day moving average is the average of prices of past 8 days. It smoothens the prices and gives a broad indication to the direction of the price movement. Moving average can be of several types, such as, simple, exponential, weighted, triangular, variable and volume adjusted etc.   Simple and exponential moving averages are most commonly used. Simple average is based on arithmetic sum of prices over n-periods, assigning equal weight to each price. 20, 50,100 and 200 day moving averages (DMA) are most popular. In exponential moving average (EMA) more weight is assigned to the recent price for example, a 10-period EMA applies an 7.18% (2/(n+1), where n is number of periods) weight to the most recent price and a 20 period EMA applies 5.52% weight to the most recent price (2/(20+1) = .0952). Notice that the weight for the shorter time period is more than the weight for the longer time period. In fact, the weight drops by half with the doubling of the period. This type of moving average reacts faster to recent price changes than a simple moving average. The 12- and 26-day EMAs are the most popular short-term averages, and the 50- and 200-day EMAs are used as signals of long-term trends. The following figure shows 20, 50 and 200 simple DMAs and 20 day EMA in the Daily chart of ICICI Bank. Note that 20 day EMA (DEMA) (shown in long dotted lines) is more responsive to the recent price change and moves closure to the price chart. It smoothens price movement and indicates the direction. Directional change of 20 EMA can be used to enter / exit the stock.

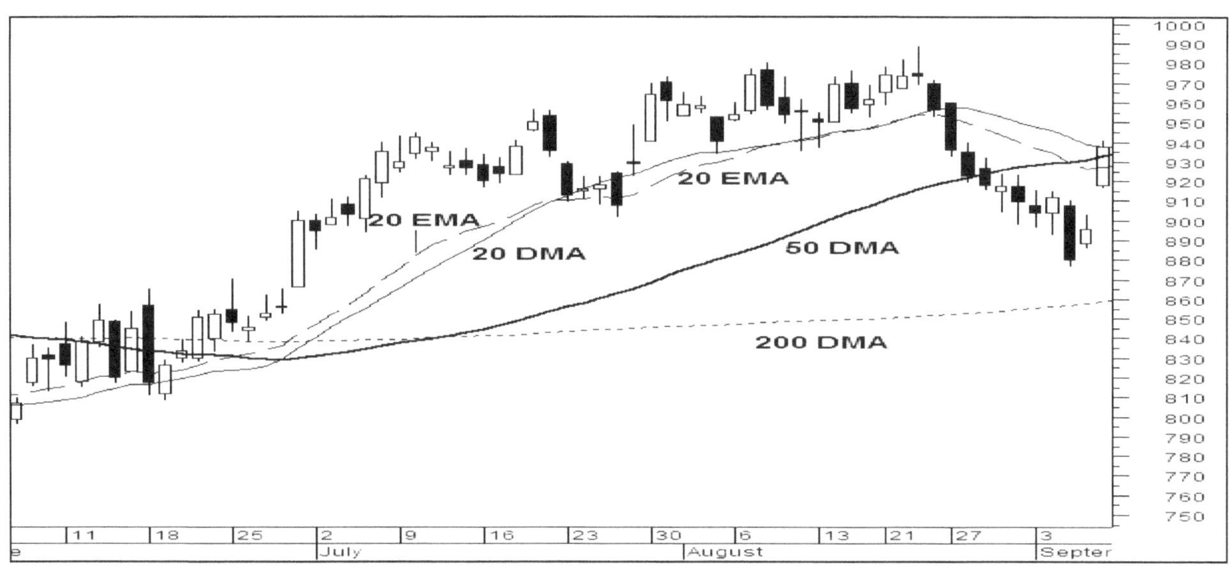

Fig. Daily chart of ICICI Bank showing 20 DMA, 20 DEMA, 50 DMA and 200 DMA

(c) Moving Averages Crossover

It is the crossover of short term and long term moving averages say (30, 100) and (50, 200) day moving averages. 50,200 DMA crossover is very popular and signals a long term breakout. If the short term moving average (50 DMA) crosses the long term moving average (200 DMA) from below and the long term moving average is upward, it indicates a definite up trend. In case the reverse is true, that is, short term moving average crosses the long term moving average from above, it signals a long term down trend. Shorter pairs of moving averages, say 30, 100 and 7, 21 DMA will indicate medium and short term up or down trends respectively. In the daily cart of Biocon (see Fig. below) 30 and 100 DMAs cross at points A and B. 30 DMA crossing 100 DMA from above (point A), signals down trend. Point B is just the opposite when 30 DMA   crosses 100 DMA from below, indicating up trend.

Fig - Daily chart of Biocon showing 30, 100 DMA crossovers [Chart created in Metastock]

Moving averages, as trend indicators pose two problems, one they are lagging indicators, that is, they signal a trend after some time delay as the formation of moving average takes time after the trend sets in, second in case of sideways movement of the price, they are subject to whipsaws due to many crossovers.

(d) Moving Average Convergence Divergence (MACD)

MACD is one of the most well known and used indicators in technical analysis. This indicator is comprised of two exponential moving averages, which help to measure momentum in the security. The MACD is simply the difference between these two moving averages plotted against a centerline. The centerline is the point at which the two moving averages are equal. Along with the MACD and the centerline, an exponential moving average of the MACD itself is plotted on the chart. It measures the short-term momentum compared to longer term momentum to find the current direction of momentum; in other words it is the difference between short and long term moving averages:

MACD = shorter term moving average- longer term moving average

When the MACD is positive, it suggests upward momentum. The opposite holds true when the MACD is negative - this suggests downward momentum. When the MACD line crosses over the centerline, it signals a crossing in the moving averages. The most common moving average values used in the calculation are the 26-day and 12-day exponential moving averages. The signal line is commonly created by using a nine-day exponential moving average of the MACD value. The short and long term values can be adjusted to meet the needs of the technician and the security. For more volatile securities, shorter term averages are used while less volatile securities should have longer averages. Another aspect to the MACD indicator is MACD histogram. The histogram is plotted on the centerline and represented by bars. Each bar is the difference between the MACD and the signal line. The higher the bars, the more is the momentum in the direction in which the bars point. The crossing of MACD (solid line) and the signal line (dotted line) (generally 9 day exponential moving average) generates buy / sell signal; when the MACD crosses the signal line from below, it generates buy signal while the crossing of signal line by MACD line from above generates sell signal (See below the daily chart of KEC International).

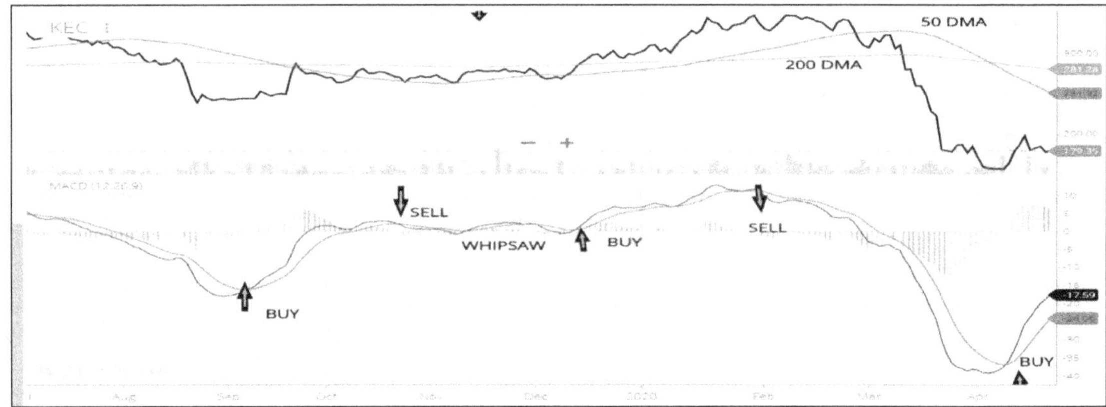

Fig. Daily chart of KEC international [chart created in Zerodha.com]

Like Moving Average Crossover, MACD suffers from two draw backs, one it generates buy/ sell signals after some time delay and second it is subject to whipsaws in non-trending zone (period of August in chart of Tata Steel). It also generates many buy and sell signals in the consolidation phase. Moving average crossovers and MACD are the most popular non-range bound indicators. These work best in trending zones, that is, when the market or the stock has a well defined up or down trend.

(e) Bollinger Bands

Bollinger Bands consist of a middle band with two outer bands. The middle band is a simple moving average that is usually set at 20 periods. The outer bands are usually set 2 standard deviations above and below the middle band. Users can change the parameters to suit their charting needs. Bollinger Bands (50, 2.1) can be used for a longer timeframe and Bollinger Bands (10, 1.9) can be used for a shorter time frame.

The bands are a measure of the volatility and automatically widen when volatility increases and narrow down when volatility decreases. When a security's price is moving in a narrow range, the Bollinger bands will constrict. This would mean that the prices are consolidating before a big move ahead. A move to the upper band shows strength, while a sharp move to the lower band shows weakness. In a strong uptrend, prices usually fluctuate between the upper band and the 20-day moving average (center line). Prices can touch the upper band at numerous points during a strong uptrend. When that happens, a crossing below the 20-day moving average warns of a trend reversal to the downside. Similarly in a strong down trend the prices fluctuate between the center and the lower band and a crossing above center line signals a trend reversal. Fig below shows the daily chart of SAIL with Bollinger Bands and RSI.

Fig.– Daily chart of SAIL showing Bollinger Bands [Chart created in Metastock]

The following observations can be made from this chart:

(i) Price chart crosses the middle band from below on 12th Sept '12, 30th Nov '12 and 18th April '13 generating BUY signals (shown by upward arrows). These are confirmed by RSI crossing the neutral line from below. (ii) Price chart crosses the middle band from above on 9th Oct '12 and 14th Jan '13 generating SELL signals (shown by downward arrows). These are confirmed by RSI crossing the neutral line from above. (iii) During the periods from 12th Sept '12 through 9th Oct '12 and from 30th Nov '12 through 14th Jan '13 the prices remain in the upper band. They pierce the upper band at a few points showing strong momentum supported by strong volumes, suggestive of possible trend reversal. (iv) During the periods from 9th Oct '12 through 30th Nov '12 and from 30th Nov '12 through 14th April '13 the prices confine to the lower band, except for a small whipsaw in the first period. (v) Trend reversal is seen near narrow bands shown by rectangles).

(2) Range Bound Indicators

Range bound indicators are bound within a range of 0 to 100.The following are the most popular range bound indicators:

(a) Relative Strength Index

Relative strength index (RSI) is most used and well known momentum indicators in technical analysis. RSI helps to signal overbought and oversold conditions in a stock. The indicator is plotted in a range between zero and 100. A reading above 70 indicates that a stock is overbought, while a reading below 30 indicates that it is oversold. This indicator helps traders to identify whether a security's price has been unreasonably pushed to high or low levels and whether a reversal is imminent. The standard calculation for RSI uses 14 trading days as the basis, which can be adjusted to meet the needs of the user. Shorter period will make RSI more volatile, making it suitable for shorter term trades.

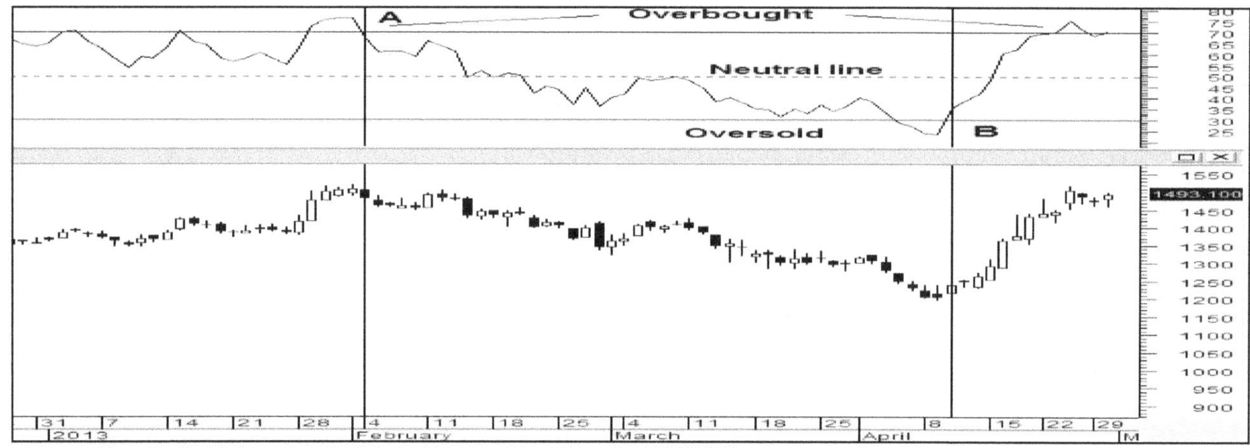

Fig -Daily Price chart of Axis Bank with 14 period RSI [Chart created in Metastock]

Above Fig. shows daily chart of Axis Bank with RSI. Note that the stock enters into bought zone on 29th January and leaves it on 4th February (point A). The stock price falls until 9th April. Its RSI moves into oversold territory on 4th April and stays there until 9th April (point B). These points (A and B) coincide with peak and bottom of stock price respectively. The trader who has taken a long position can exit at point A when the stock moves out of overbought zone. He or she can take a fresh long position at point B when RSI moves out of oversold zone.

(b) Stochastic Oscillator

Stochastic is one of the most recognized momentum indicators used in technical analysis. It is plotted within a range of zero and 100 and signals overbought conditions above 80 and oversold conditions below 20. The stochastic oscillator contains two lines. The first line is the %K, which is the raw measure used to formulate momentum behind the oscillator. The second line is the %D, which is simply a moving average of the %K. The %D line is considered to be the more important of the two lines as it produces better signals. Some chartists use only %D line to represent stochastic oscillator. The oscillator generally uses the past 14 trading periods but can be adjusted to meet the needs of the user; a short term trader may use smaller period.

Fig. Daily chart of Maruti with Stochastic %K and %D lines [Chart created in icharts.in]

Above Figure shows daily chart of Maruti with Raw Stochastic (%K line, thick curve) and its 3 day moving average (%D line, thin curve). The stochastic moved into oversold zone (<20) in February end when the stock was continuously falling. It bottomed out on 1st March when %K line started moving up but remained below neutral line (50) and again entered oversold zone. The up move began on 4th April when %K line move out of oversold zone. Since then the up move is continuing with %K line entering overbought over bought territory. This is confirmed by crossing of the price chart with 30 DMA. The trader can take long position when the stochastic moves above neutral line and exit when it moves out of overbought zone. Similarly short position can be taken when stochastic crosses neutral line from above and remain short until it remains below neutral line or moves out of oversold zone.

2.5 Divergence

Divergence is a situation that occurs when stock price and an indicator like its RSI, MACD or Stochastic Oscillator in a chart move in opposite directions. Traders often look for divergences by comparing a stock's direction to the direction of its RSI, MACD or Stochastic Oscillator. Implication of divergence is that this price movement is not sustainable and reversal in stock price is likely to take place soon; the price following the direction of the indicator. It is a key reversal signal. There are two kinds of divergences: positive and negative. Positive divergence occurs when the indicator moves higher while the stock is declining. Negative divergence occurs when the indicator moves lower while the stock is rising. The chart of Titan Industries (Fig below) shows positive divergence between stock price and MACD in April '13 (thick slanting black lines in the chart). It implies that owing to strong positive momentum in MACD, the decline in stock's price is unsustainable and stock finally moves up.

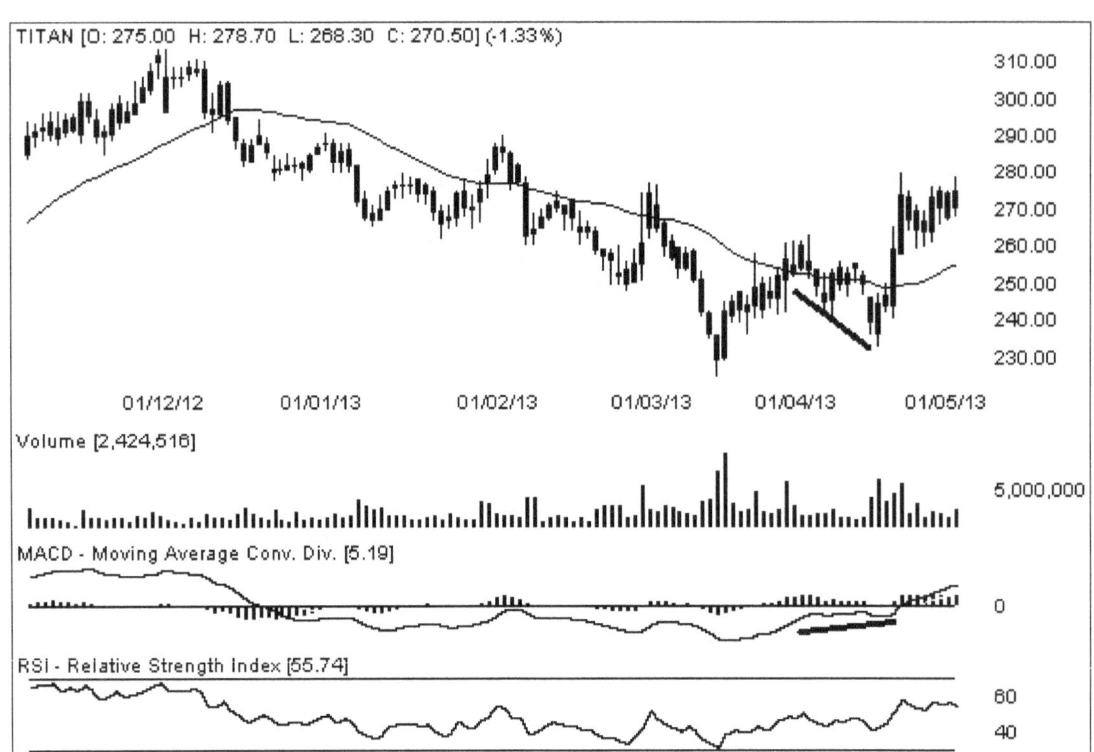

Fig : Chart of Titan Industries showing positive divergence with MACD [Chart created in Metastock]

The chart of RCOM (Fig. below) shows negative divergence with RSI (thick slanting black lines in the chart) Due to high negative momentum in RSI, the rise in stocks price in the month of January is not sustainable and hence fall in the price.

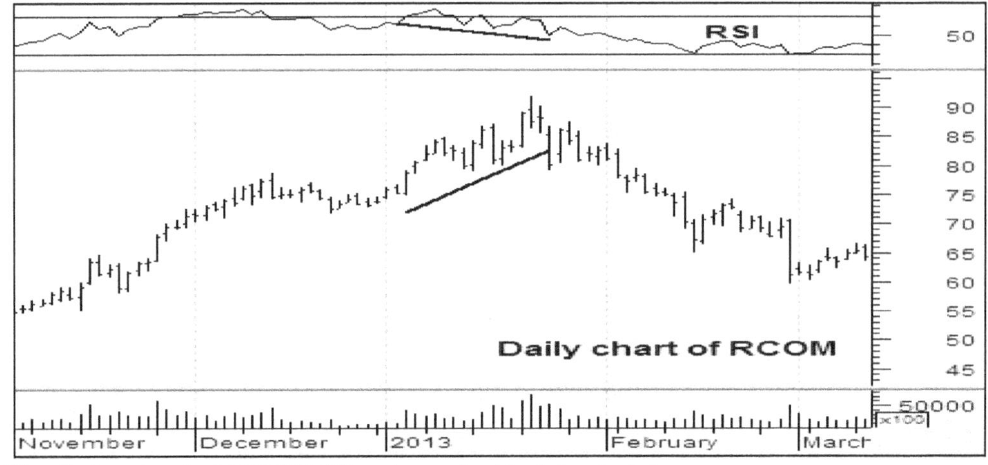

Fig: Daily chart of RCOM [Chart created in icharts.in]

The divergences can be seen in other indicators too. Examples of divergence with CCI and OBV indicators are given in the above sections.

2.6 Combining the Indicators

As discussed in the above section no technical indicator is 100% failsafe; they need to be confirmed with some other indicator(s) of different kind. For this reason we use two or more indicators together in technical analysis. Most commonly used indicators are: Moving averages, MACD, RSI, Stochastic and Volume. Various combinations of moving averages such as (7, 20), (10, 30), (20, 50), (30, 100), (50, 200) days are commonly used depending on short, medium and long term analysis. Intraday traders use 5 minute or 30 minute charts depending on their aggressiveness. Long term investors use weekly or even monthly charts. The following examples illustrate the use of these indicators:

Example 1 - ICICI Bank: Look at the following chart of ICICI Bank (Fig. below). The following points can be observed:

(1) The stock was in uptrend until 20th February when it broke the supporting trend line. MACD gave an earlier breakout signal on 8th February. RSI, being a leading indicator gave still earlier signal on 1st February by crossing neutral line. Stochastic oscillator also gave a confirmed bearish signal on 5th February by entering in oversold zone.

(2) The stock entered in the down channel on 21st February. It broke out the resistance line on 16th April. The downtrend was confirmed earlier by MACD on 18th April, RSI on 15th April by crossing neutral line and still earlier on 9th April by Stochastic by crossing of %D line with %K line from below. A long term trader/ investor can use trend line and MACD whereas a short term trader should use RSI or still better Stochastic for faster trades.

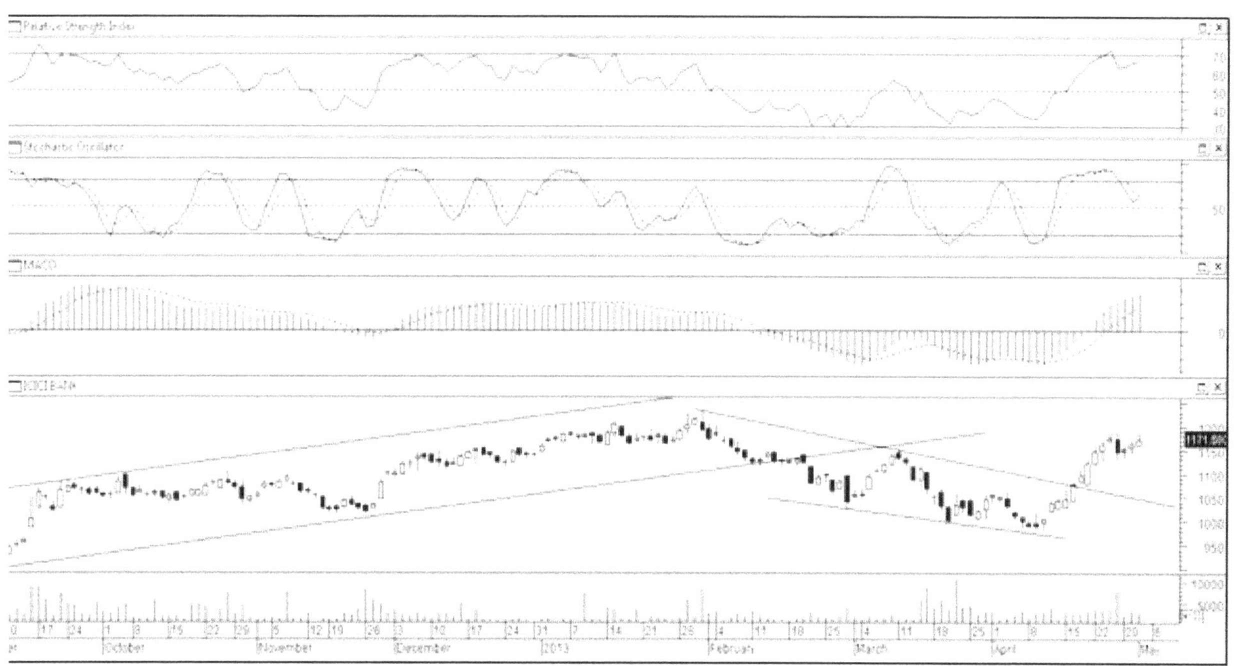

Fig : Daily chart of ICICI Bank with multiple indicators. [Chart created in Metastock]

Example 2- Opto Circuits: Observe the weekly chart of Opto Circuits (Fig. below}

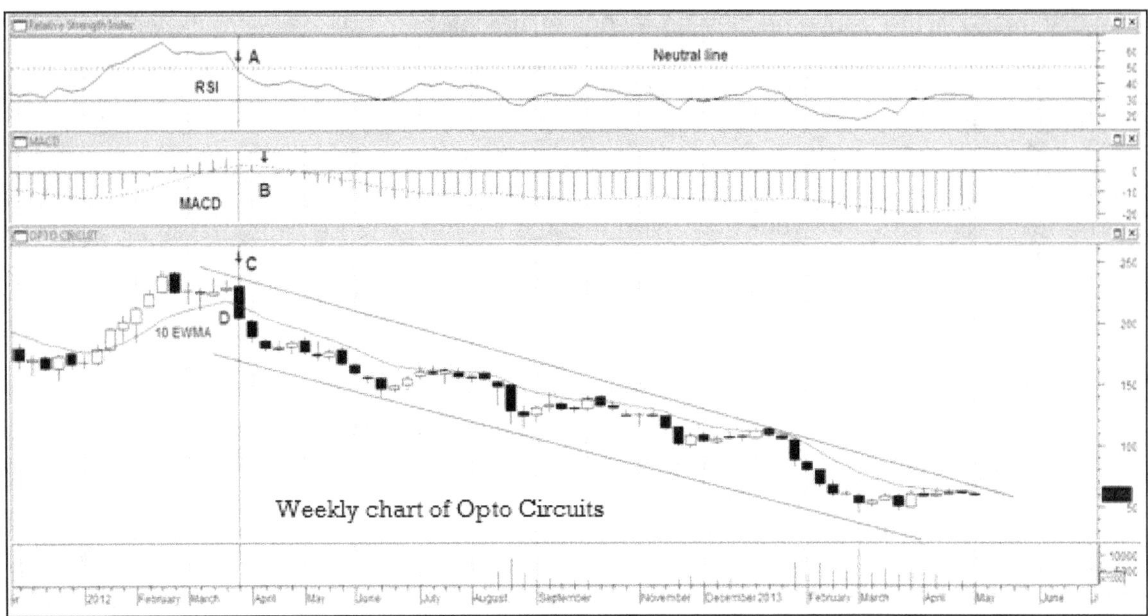

Fig - Weekly chart of Opto Circuits [Chart created in Metastock]

The price of Opto Circuits fell by 75% from the peak of 230 on 30th March '12 to the low of 58 on 3rd May '7. The stock since then is moving in a down channel. A passive investor holding the stock in the hope of revival would have lost heavily. Exit strategy is therefore is very important in the stock market. Let us post mortem the chart to find out the lost opportunity of selling the stock. A closer analysis of the chart would reveal the following selling points:

- A sell signal was generated by RSI on 30th March '13 when it moved below neutral line (point A in the chart). Price of stock at this point was Rs 203.
- MACD generated sell signal on 13th April '13 when MACD signal became and moved into negative territory (point B in the chart). Price at this point was Rs 175.
- A sell signal was generated by the long black candle formed on 30th March '12, which engulfed the white candle formed on 30th March '12 (point C in the chart). It was subsequently confirmed by three black crows. Price at this point was Rs 203.
- A sell signal was generated by turning down of rising 10 period exponential moving average on 23rd March '12 (point D in the chart). Price at this point was Rs 225.

The stock is still moving in down channel and there is no sign of trend reversal at least for now as MACD is negative and RSI is much below neutral line. A finer picture can be seen in daily chart shown below (Fig. below).

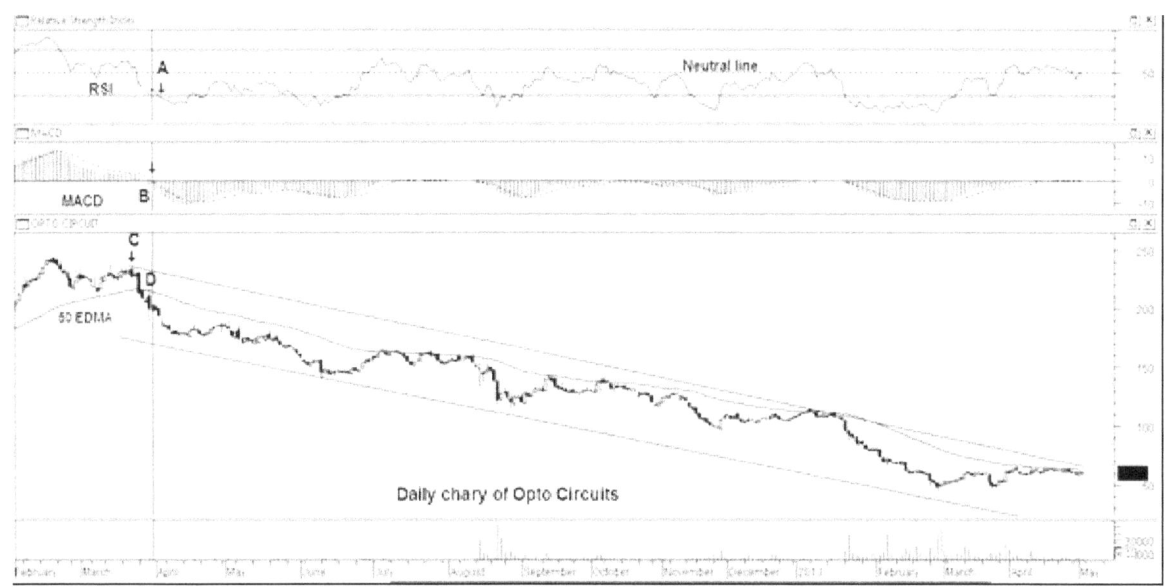

Fig- Daily chart of Opto Circuits [Chart created in Metastock]

There is only slight change in picture. Selling points are slightly shifted as follows:

Point	Indicator	Date	Price in Rs
A	RSI crossing neutral line	4th April '12	194
B	MACD crossing zero line	30th March '12	203
C	Bearish candle engulfing	22nd March '12	227
D	50 day EMA turning downwards	27th March '12	208

Here also there is no sign of trend reversal as RSI is hovering around neutral line and MACD signal is near zero. Down channel is also intact. Uptrend will begin when the stock will cross resistance line with heavy volume. The earliest up trend signal will be generated by RSI or Stochastic.

2.7 Retracement Levels

In case of a down market the traders are in a dilemma as to the extent of correction. It is here that retracement theory is of help. It seeks to find the likely levels from where the prices may retrace their path. According to Fibonacci retracement theory the prices may falls to the following three levels:

- First level is 33.2% correction, or retracement of the original price move,
- Second level is 50% correction, or retracement of the original price move and
- Third level is 61.8% correction, or retracement of the original price move.

As an example suppose a stock has risen from a level of 100 to peak of 200, thus making a rise (up move) of 100. The above three retracement levels can be computed as follows:

Level 1 = peak price – 33.2% of rise = 200-33.2 =161.8
Level 2 = peak price – 50.2% of rise = 200-50   =150
Level 3 = peak price – 61.8% of rise = 200-61.8 =133.2

Fig. below shows retracement levels in the chart of Arvind Mills. The stock takes transient support at 23.6%, 33.2%, 50% and slightly below 61.8% levels. The last level suggests exhaustion of the down fall.

Fig - Retracement levels in the chart of Arvind Mills

2.8 Strategies for the Long Term Investor

As commonly believed, fundamental analysis is for the long term investor and technical analysis is for the short term trader. Contrary to this belief technical analysis can also be equally applied to longer term time frames of weeks and months to help investors in identifying the right entry and exit points. Knowledge of trend line, moving averages and certain key indicators can of immense help in identification of buy and sell timings. Some investors use technical analysis to validate fundamentals of a security to rule out the possibility of manipulation of balance sheet. In fact the fundamentals of a company are discounted in its price.

Technical analysis for long term investors is slightly different than for short term traders. Long term investors use weekly and monthly charts to see broader picture and ignore short term movements called noise. The following parameters are quite useful in long term analysis: Support and resistance lines, 200 DMA, 200/50 DMA crossover, MACD, weekly oscillators like RSI, Stochastic or

William's %R. The following examples demonstrate the application of technical analysis for longer period time frames which are useful for long term investors:

Example 1- Infosys Technologies: Fig. below shows monthly chart of Infosys Technologies.

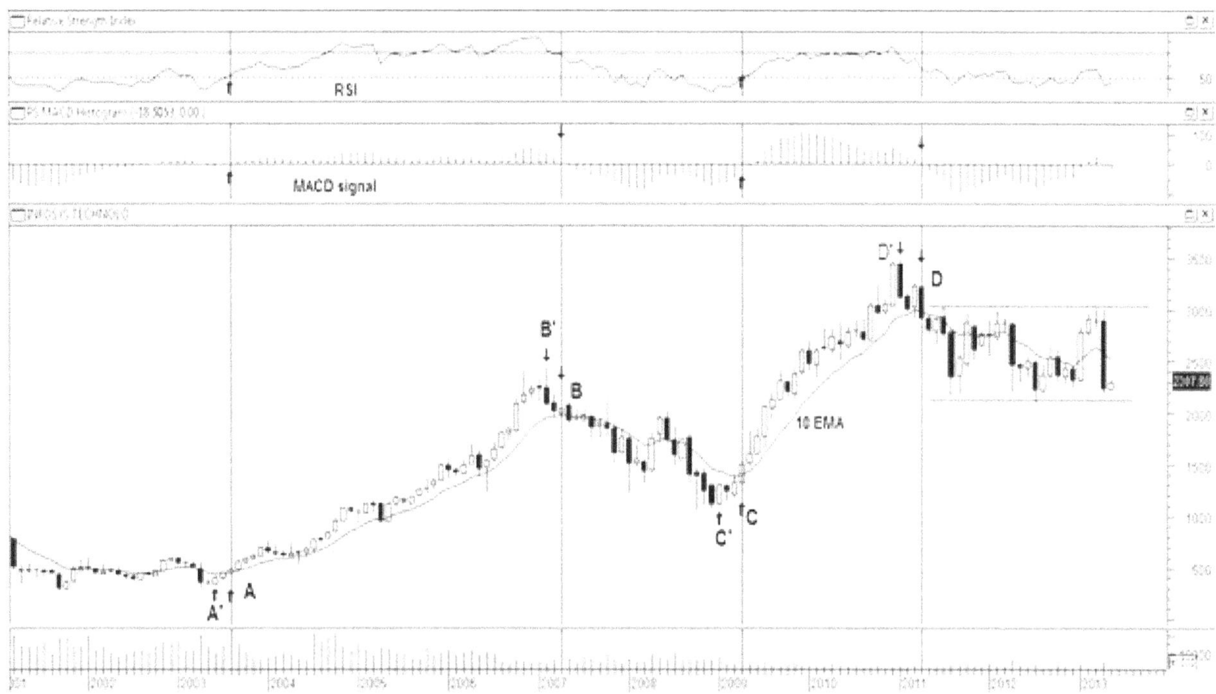

Fig - Monthly chart of Infosys Technologies [Chart created in Metastock]

Using this chart the investor could have identified the following BUY and SELL opportunities:

Date	Point on the chart	Indicator(s)	Action	Price
29th August '03	A	MACD signal, RSI crossing neutral line	BUY	489
30th April '07	B	MACD signal	SELL	2049
29th April '09	C	MACD signal, RSI crossing neutral line	BUY	1507
29th April '11	D	MACD signal	SELL	2906

The stock came out from consolidation at point A and remained in uptrend until point B when it went in downtrend. The downtrend continued until point C when uptrend began. This uptrend continued until point D when it started moving sideways. The stock is still moving in a horizontal channel with big monthly swings. Candles gave early signals as shown in the table below:

Date	Point on the chart	Indicator(s)	Action	Price
30th June '03	A'	Morning star	BUY	408
28th February '07	B'	Evening star	SELL	2078
30th January '09	C'	Bullish engulfing	BUY	1305
31st January '11	D'	Dark cloud cover	SELL	3116

Example 2- Alok Industries: Fig. below shows weekly chart of Alok Industries from January 2007 to April 2007. The stock fell from a peak of 104 on 4th January '03. It broke the resistance line R1 on 12th December '08 arresting the fall at Rs15. Since then it has been in a long term downtrend making minor unsustainable rallies. It could not breach 200 WMA line. It is currently moving in a narrow down channel R2 S1 showing no sign of up move. The investor should have got out of the stock soon after the beginning of the steep fall in January '08 as signalled by crossing of MACD average (dotted line) with MACD (bars) on 25th January '08 from above (point A in the chart).

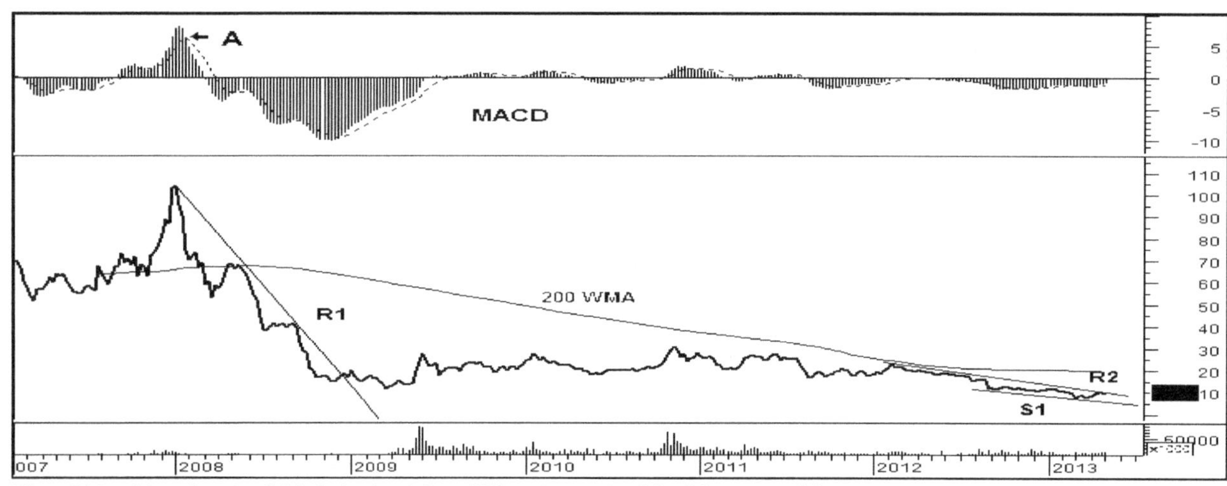

Fig - Weekly chart of Alok Industries [Chart created in Metastock]

-------------oOoOoOo-------------

Chapter 3

STUDYING

MARKET CONDITIONS

"Holding for long term works beautifully well in a bull market. In a bear market it can be absolutely disastrous"
– *Richard Russell*

"

3.1 Introduction

The lure of stock market attracts many people. Many novice investors enter the market at a wrong time and lose their hard earned money. The stock markets are highly volatile and often choppy, many small investors/ traders get lost in the stock market jungle. There is a saying in the stock market "***Bulls Make Money***, ***Bears Make Money and Pigs Get Slaughtered***". You must equip yourself with the proper arsenal before taking big moves in the market. Before buying the securities it is necessary to study the market conditions. Stock market movement is greatly impacted by the county's economy which moves in cycles. The overall economy affects business which also moves in cycles. The following section describes business cycles and their effect on stocks.

3.2 Business Cycles

Business cycles move through three general phases Early, Middle and Late that accompany GO and STOP signs for the stock market. These phases are depicted in the following diagram (Fig 3.1):

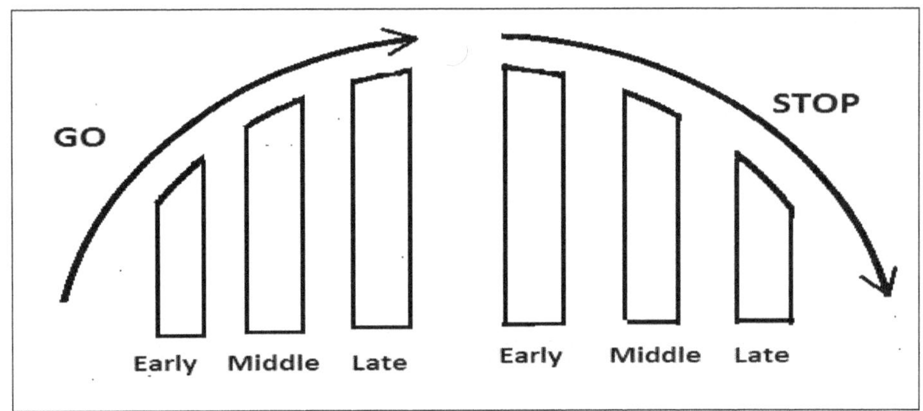

Fig 3.1- Phases of Business Cycles

Business cycle phases create conditions in which certain stock sectors perform better than others. The following table (Table 3.1) shows the sectors performing in these phases:

Table 3.1- Business Cycle Phases and Sectors

Business Cycle	Phase	Sectors
GO	Early	Financial, Technology
	Middle	Technology, Basic Materials, Transportation, Industrials
	Late	Energy, FMCG, Health Care
STOP	Early	Health care, Staples, Utilities
	Middle	Utilities, Bonds
	Late	Bonds, Real estate, Financial

Smart investors move through the progression of these sectors and exit the previous sectors. Institutional investors like FIIs, DIIs and Fund managers invest more heavily in companies that provide goods and services associated with the current phase of business cycle.

3.3 Phases of Stock Market

As mentioned earlier that the market moves in the following three distinct phases:

(a) Upwards or bullish: A bull market is associated with increasing investor confidence, and increased investing in anticipation of future price increases. A bullish trend in the stock market often begins before the general economy shows clear signs of recovery. Here bulls (who believe that market will rise) dominate the market. The market moves up because people see that economy is good and companies are performing better. The market moves up because of excess liquidity and greater amount of money being deployed in the stock market. SENSEX was in a bull market trend for about five years from April 2003 to January 2008 as it increased from 2,900 points to 21,000 points. FIIs take keen interest in bull market and pump in money. Retail investors participation also increases.

(b) Downwards or bearish: A bear market is a general decline in the stock market over a period of time. It is a transition from high investor optimism to widespread investor fear and pessimism Here bears dominate the market. The market is down because people see that economy is in bad shape and going in recession. Companies' performance becomes poor, productivity and consumption figures are down. FIIs lose interest and take out money from the market. Money from the stock market moves to other asset classes like gold, real estate and debt. The most recent example occurred between January 2008 and March 2009, when Sensex crashed by 62% as a result of the global sub-prime financial crisis.

(c) Sideways or consolidation: Here bull and bear both are equal players. The market loses momentum   and remains sideways in a narrow range for quite sometime until the economy starts improving. Long-term investors get of the market and there are small movements due activity of traders. The market becomes indecisive and it turns out to be a trader's play.

It is, therefore, necessary for the investor to recognize the health and direction of the market. For an investor beginning of bull phase is the time to buy and make money. The early entrants are the biggest gainers. The investor must exit or sell major chunk of his/ her equities as soon as the market trend changes to downwards and move his / her money to debt. He /she should then wait for economy to improve and stock market coming out consolidation and again start investing in good performing large caps. When the large cap shares have attained full value, the investor can move to good midcaps. But he /she should avoid buying small cap stocks unless he / she is sure about their performance. In case of bearish phase the small caps will be the first to fall followed by mid caps and the large caps will be the last to fall.

An investor must monitor the performance of stocks held in his/ her portfolio and the stocks in the watch list on daily / weekly basis. Some simple rules can be followed by investors / traders:

1. Watch charts daily after market closing
2. Watch charts again and again to find finer points like TV replay of cricket match.
3. For trading: use weekly charts to identify the underlying trend.
           : use daily chart to see breakout.
           : use 5/30 min chart for making entries and exits
3. For long term investing: use weekly charts for finding long term support and resistance areas.
4.   Make trend your friend and ride the momentum. Enter the stock as soon as trend becomes positive and quit as soon as the reversal of trend takes place.

3.4 Market Direction by Technical Indicators

The direction of the market can be judged by the use of technical indicators. Technical indicators are broadly classified in two categories:

1. Trend following or lagging like MA and MACD
2. Oscillators or leading indicators like momentum, RSI, Stochastics oscillator and William's % R.

Before deciding about which type of indicator to use, it is necessary to know the kind of market namely, trending or trading. A trading market is when the index moves sideways within a range. It is also called consolidation phase. A trending market is either up (bullish) identified by higher tops and higher bottoms or down (bearish) making lower tops and lower bottoms. In a trending market it is further necessary to determine strength of the market before making any move. Strength of the market can be determined by use of Average Directional Index (ADX).

(i) Average Directional Index (ADX)

It has been described earlier in the chapter on Technical Analysis. Some key points related to judging the direction of market are recapitulated here. High readings of ADX above 40, indicate a strong trend and low readings below 20, indicate a weak trend. When this indicator is showing a low reading, then a trading range is likely to develop. Investors should avoid stocks with low readings. They should look for stocks that have high readings. Extremely high readings signal end of trend. Very few stocks are seen with the ADX above 50. Once it gets that high, you start to see trends coming to an end and trading ranges developing again. You should, however, become cautious for trend reversal when ADX reaches 40. ADX should be used for scanning stocks in strong up or down trend and also for filtering out stocks in narrow sideways range. Further as with other indicators, ADX alone is not failsafe, ADX signal must be confirmed by other indicators.

Directional indicator is a momentum indicator that helps quantify the trending behaviour of a stock. There are two directional indicators +DI (positive) and –DI (negative) indicators. ADX is derived from these indicators (+DI and –DI). A common use of the +DI and –DI indicators is the crossover trading signal approach. This means that when the +DI line crosses the -DI line from below, a buy signal is generated. When the –DI crosses the +DI from below a sell signal is generated. Because the Directional Indicators are quite volatile, crossover signals must be confirmed by other indicators and price breakouts to avoid false signals. Another approach is to further smooth the +DI and –DI with a moving average, this reduces some of the false signals. ADXR or just ADR is smoothened version of ADX. The following examples illustrate the use of ADX and ADR:

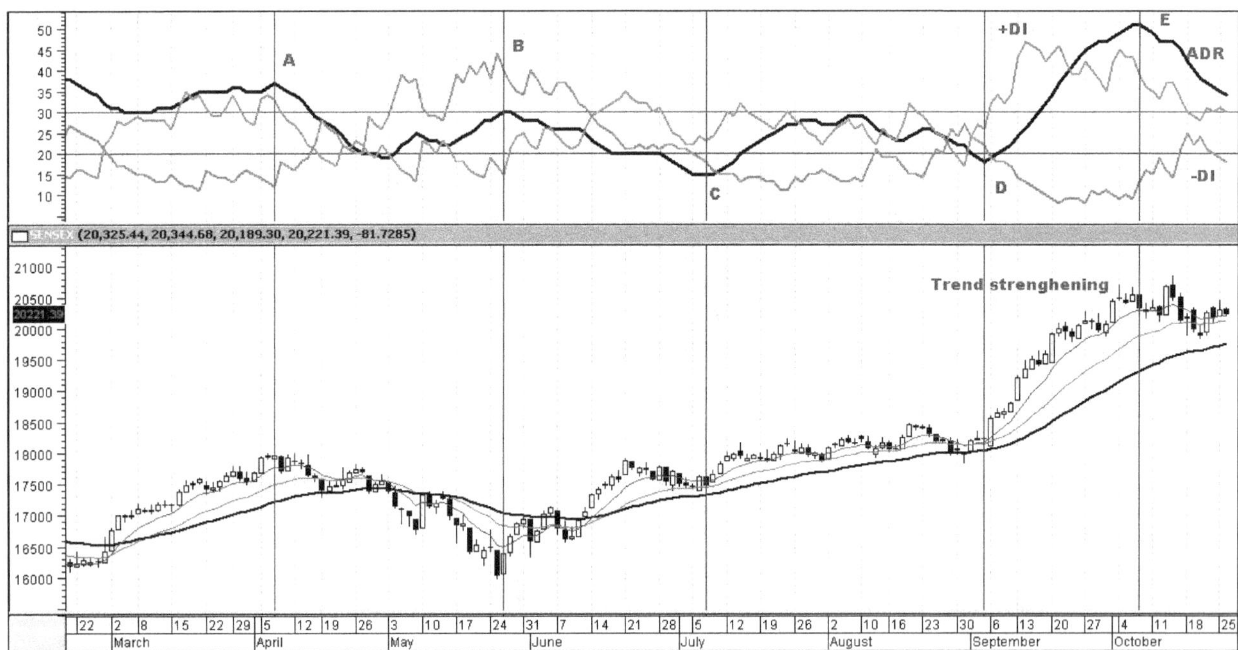

Fig 3.2 Sensex chart showing ADR

way to judge the trend, its strength and reversal. Trend lines are an important tool for both trend identification In the above chart (Fig 3.2) of Sensex from March to October 2010, ADR (thick black curve) changes the direction at points A, B, C, D and E, so does the Sensex. When ADR lies between the range 20-30 (from 15 July to 2 Sept) the market, i.e., the Sensex moves in a trading range. The rise of ADR above 30 on Sept 18 indicates strengthening of trend. This is also confirmed by 8 day short term moving average curve (green curve) moving up after touching the 20 day long term moving average curve (red curve). Abnormal rise of ADX to 50 signals trend reversal to consolidation. It can also be seen that Sensex is up when +DI (green curve) is above –DI (red curve) and it moves downwards when –DI is above –DI.

(ii) Trend Lines

Trend lines offer the simplest and confirmation. Trend lines also help identify support and resistance levels. You should make trend your friend and enjoy profits so long as the trend is up and sell sooner the upward trend loses steam and falls flat or reverses. In the trading or consolidation range there are many whipsaws and no clear trend exists. It is the time to trade.

A trend line connects a series of two or more high or low points of the price chart. More the number of lows or tops it touches, more valid it is. You can draw trend lines on the chart quite easily just by visual observation. It should touch at least 2 or more lows or highs. Some software packages draw the trend lines automatically.

The trend line joining the lows is also the support line. When the price chart pierces it, it signals the trend reversal and time to sell. The trend line joining the highs is called resistance line. When the price chart breaks line upward, it is the time to buy. The following chart (Fig 3.3) demonstrates the major trends, trend lines and trend reversals on the Nifty chart:

Fig 3.3- Daily 1 year chart of Nifty showing Trend Lines

In the daily chart of Nifty from May 2012 to May 2013 (Fig 3.8) three trends can be seen (1) upward from 4th June '12 to 8th Feb'13, (2) down from 8th Feb '13 to 12th April '13 and (3) up from 12th April '7. The downtrend begins at point B with piercing of the support trend line AB. Fresh uptrend begins from point F with upward breakout of resistance line. Lines AB, EB and EF are support lines whereas lines CD, FG and HI are resistance lines. Trend reversal takes place on violation of support line in case of uptrend and on that of resistance line in case of down trend.

(iii) Moving Average

A long term (200 Day Simple Moving Average) can be used to judge market direction and to generate buy/ sell signals. This simple technique works well for most trending markets/ stocks but generates somewhat delayed signals. It can be successfully used by long term investors. The following examples illustrate this point:

Fig 3.4: 10 year Sensex chart showing 40 week moving average

In the above 10 year weekly chart of Sensex (Fig 3.4) 40 WMA (smooth line) serves as indicator of market direction. In the 10 year interval from 2003 through 2013 the market changed direction 4 times (at points B, C, D and E). These points could be used as entry / exit points by a long term investor.

(iv) Moving Average Crossovers

Short term and long term moving average (MA) crossovers are indicative of trend change. One can choose MA pairs like (3, 8); (8, 22); (10, 30); (20, 50) or (50, 200) days depending on his/ her level of activity. An active short term trader would choose (3, 8) day MA pair where as a long term investor would prefer (50,200) day MA pair. Moving average smoothens the price chart; their crossovers indicate change of direction of price. MA crossovers are lagging indicators as they give a signal only after the event gas taken place. In case of a trading market, when there is no clear trend, MAs suffer from whipsaws, during periods of whipsaws MA crossovers are of little value in indication of market direction. MAs work best in trending markets. The following chart of Nifty (Fig 3.5) will illustrate these points:

Fig 3.5 -10 year weekly chart of Nifty

The above chart shows moving average crossover of 10 and 30 period moving averages. The first up trend begins on 17th September '04 with the crossing of 10 period EMA with 30 period EMA from below and continues until 7th March '08 with the crossing 10 period EMA with 30 period from above, signaling a down trend. The downtrend persists until 8th May '09. Nifty then remains in uptrend until 28th January '11. Now the moving averages enter into whipsaws until 3rd August '12, expect for the short period of down trend. The final uptrend commences from 3rd August '12. Note that touching of the two moving averages inside a definite trend shows the strength of the trend, as on 18th April '07. Upward and downward arrows indicate possible BUY and SELL points respectively.

3.5 Market Direction by Fundamental Factors

(i) Price Earning Ratio (PER)

Nifty or stock price is a direct function of the earnings, higher the earnings higher the price. In fact the Nifty moved in a PER band (Fig 3.6), during the period 2000 through 2012 it has remained in a PE band of 12 to 29 with the median value of 17.5. When PER of Nifty is abnormally high (above 23, it signals that the market is ripe for correction and when it is too low (near 12), it is ready to move up. An investor should remember these turning points for change of market direction.

Fig 3.6: Nifty PER chart [source https://craytheon.com/]

The following table (3.2) shows the market valuation. Investors can conveniently hold stocks during the Sensex forward PER value between 14 to 22.

Table 3.2-Market valuation

Nifty PER	<12	12 – 18	18 -20	20-24	24-28	>28
Implication	Grossly undervalued	Undervalued	Fair valued	Overvalued	Grossly overvalued	Bubble formation

It is further seen from Nifty PER chart (see Fig. 3.6) that when Nifty PER crosses above 29, market peaks and when Nifty PER falls below 16, market bottoms out and is ready to move. According to one study, investing at PER less than 14 produced a year Nifty return of 152% while investing at PER between 24-30 produced -33% to -40%% returns (see table 3.3 below):

Table 3.3-Nifty PER and 3 year return

Nifty PER	<14	14-16	16-18	18-20	20-22	22-24	24-26	26-28	28-30
3 year return %	152	112	79	51	21	-15	-33	-37	- 40

Based on historical data investors can safeguard their investment portfolio and earn handsome profit by following the investment rationale suggested in the following table (Table 3.4):

Table 3.4- Investment Rationale

Nifty PER range	25-30	20-25	15-20	12-15	<12
Valuation	Very	Expensive	Average	Cheap	Very

	expensive				cheap
Investment Decision	Screaming sell	Sell	Buy or Hold	Buy	Screaming buy

(ii) Foreign Institutional Investor (FII) Fund Flow

Indian stock markets have been highly dependent on FII fund flows. Over the years higher fund flows from FIIs have helped generate higher returns from Sensex. There has been a strong correlation between FII fund flow and Nifty/Sensex, Nifty rises with FII fund flow in stock market. Fig 3.7 illustrates this fact. With the FII fund flow of $8b in 2006, Sensex gave a return of 39% and in 2007 an FII fund flow of $16b gave a return of 44%. The fall of 62% in Sensex in 2008 was not due to performance of companies but due to rapid outflow of $13b due sub prime rate crisis of USA. The 85% surge in Sensex in 2009 was due to FII investment of $16b (of 2007 level). The rapid fall of 2008 gave Indian investors an excellent opportunity in invest heavily. Since then the market is on rising spree having generated a whooping return of 148% from March 2009 to January 2013, translating in a CAGR of 27%.

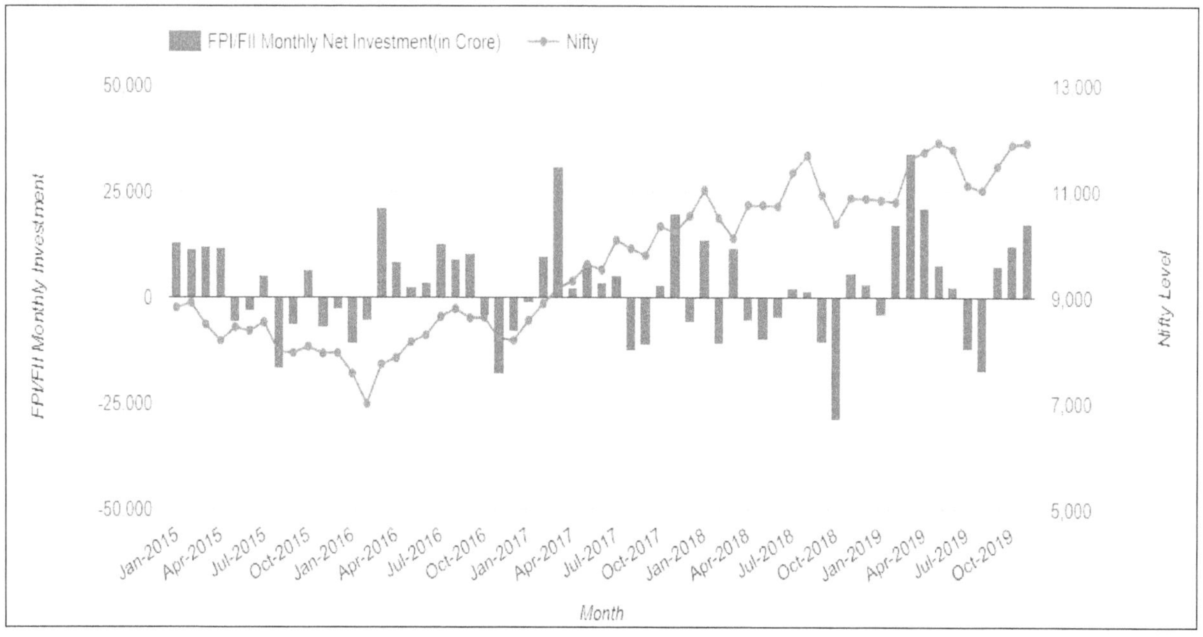

Fig 3.7- Nifty and FII fund flow [source www.equityfriend.com/]

3.5 Market Timing

As is clear from the discussion that even for a long term investor, timing the entry and exit in the stock market is crucial to good returns. A closer look to 30 year Sensex chart shown below (Fig 3.8) will illustrate this point:

Fig 3.8 – 30 year Sensex chart [Chart created in Zerodha.com]

In the 30 year period Sensex made three major up moves (shown in green colour) and two major down moves (shown in red colour). Right entry and exit points are shown by upward and downward arrows respectively. Wrong entry and exit can lead to big loss. Thus study of direction of the market is essential for success in the stock market.

3.6 Signs of Bull Market

Bull markets in stocks often coincide with periods of robust economic growth. Increased earnings often lead to higher stock prices, and a general optimism can attract more people to the stock market, increasing share prices further. At the extreme, bull markets can create bubbles in which prices rise far past the value of the underlying asset. Signs that the market is entering a phase of investor confidence are:

1. Bull markets begin before the economy starts to recover.
2. Interest rates are low.
3. Industrial production statistics are inching higher.
4. Technology and cyclical stocks are starting to rise.
5. Weekly chart of Sensex/ Nifty shows higher highs and higher lows
6. Major share indices are above 200 DMA
7. Advance/ Decline ratio is more than one.
8. MACD (Moving Average Convergence / Divergence) line is above the trigger line and rising.

Sound approach to trade in bull market is to look for fundamentally strong companies with the following characteristics:

1. With earnings that are growing faster than average.
2. In a strong sector.
3. In a growing economy while the stock is approaching a technical buy signal on its candle chart and performing better than the average stock / Sensex with high relative strength.

A bull market can slowly move to consolidation phase. In this case the major indices will be around 200 DMA, MACD will become flat or move near zero. The bull market could suddenly turn into bear market due to some untoward global or domestic event like the sudden crash of Indian stock market due to global financial crisis of 2003. The investor must remain cautious in such cases and quit the market at the earliest opportunity. It is here the indicators come handy.

3.7 Signs of Bear Market

As you invest in / trade stocks on the market, you need to identify when the market is taking a downward turn, that is, becoming a bear market. You would need to so adjust your trading strategy accordingly. Early signs of a bear market are:

1. Weakening of economic indicators, Bear markets typically begin before the economy starts to decline.
2. Deteriorating corporate earnings
3. Increasing inflation, Interest rates are rising.
4. Basic material stocks, energy stocks, and consumer staples are performing well.
5. Poor housing demand
6. Major share indices start falling below 200 DMA
7. Advance; Decline ratio is less than one.
8. Major indices Sensex/ Nifty show lower highs and lower lows
9. MACD (Moving Average Convergence / Divergence) line is below the trigger line and falling.

Your trading strategy in a bear market should be to focus on looking to sell or short fundamentally weak companies with the following characteristics:

1. With poor earnings or no earnings.
2. In a weak sector.
3. In a declining economy.
4. When the stock approaches technical sell signal on its candle chart and is performing worse than the Sensex / average stock with low relative strength.

---------OOOOOOO---------

Chapter 4

STOCK SELECTION

> One of the central problems of investing is that people focus far too much on the purchase of equities and not enough on selling them. They spend a lot of time on analysing companies and looking to buy 'value' – that is, they want to buy bargains in a market. But little time is spent in analysing when to sell 'value' – that is, when to sell assets for which risk-reward is no longer attractive. *– Marc Faber*

4.1 Importance of Sector and Stock Selection

Right stock selection and right entry and exit timings are keys to successful investing. Many investors buy stocks on the advice of the broker, friends or TV experts, hold them for long period often resulting in an unwieldy underperforming portfolio. No sector or stock is best for ever. Many best performing stocks turn sour at some point of time. Both sectors and stocks must be carefully selected. Timing their entry and exit is equally important for optimal returns.

Most broad moves of the stock market are sector driven. Nearly half of any company's stock is typically driven by the sector to which the stock belongs. Selection of the sector, therefore, is vital prior to selection of the stock. As discussed earlier, Indian economy is broadly divided into 12 major sectors according BSE indices classification, viz., IT, FMCG, Capital Goods, Consumer Durables, Healthcare, PSU, Telecom, Oil and Gas, Banks, Metals, Realty, Power and Energy. There are some other small sectors like Cement, Fertilizers, Agribusiness, Sugar, Tea, Hotels and Hospitality, Shipping, Textiles, Paints, Paper and Packaging, Logistics , Gems and Jewellery, Retail etc. Before entering stock market you must identify the strong sectors and look for good companies within these sectors. Charts of sectors are available on BSE and NSE websites. You can compare performance of all sectors and look for strong sectors or still better the turnaround sectors. After selecting the good performing sectors, you should look for the top performing stocks in each sector.

4.2 Stock screening

Stock screening is the process of searching for stocks that meet certain predetermined investment and financial criteria. Many online stock broking firms provide stock screeners. A stock screener has three components: a database of companies, a set of variables and a screening engine that finds the companies satisfying those variables to generate a list of matches. It helps   to select stocks based on a customized set of conditions and variables. For example, you may want to do a search using a screen for all those companies that have a price / earnings ratio of less than 10, an earnings growth rate of more than 15%, and a dividend yield of more than 3% or stocks above 200 DMA. You can even compare various stocks of different sectors on their fundamentals like revenues, profits, EPS, return on investment (ROI), PER, P/B ratio, market capitalization, total assets, quarterly growth etc.   It can also help you in searching undervalued stocks. Automatic stock screeners, which query a stock database to select and rank stocks according to user specified (or prespecified) criteria are also available with leading online brokers.

There are 5000+ listed companies in India and it is really difficult to analyze each company for investment. This is where Stock Screeners come in handy. They help you shortlist stocks for investment very quickly based on pre-determined or customised criteria. There are several free stock screeners for the Indian stock markets viz., www.screener.in, www.askkuber.com, www.capital4.com,   www.icicidirect.com,   www.hdfcseurities.com,   www.bullshouse.com, www.idbipaisabuilder.com, www.edelweiss.in, www.equitymaster.com.   Most of them provide several   readymade   search   screens.   www.icicidirect.com,   www.equitymaster.com, www.hdfcsecurities.com, economictimes.indiatimes.com, in.reuters.com, etc   provide a large number of readymade search screens like large, medium, small cap stocks with high price momentum, cheapest stocks of large cap companies, distressed, momentum stocks, poor man's stocks, stocks with up and down estimated earnings, future stocks, top profitable companies, medium and large cap stocks with high dividend yield and low PE ratios, outperforming sectors and technical   screeners with new highs/ lows, momentum stocks, stocks crossing above certain DMA etc .These can quickly help you select fundamentally good stocks. Technical analysis can help you identify the right entry and exit points. The following practical rules of thumb can be applied to stock screeners:

- Market cap > Rs 100 crore. Fund managers avoid small cap stocks due to uncertainty of their performance.
- PEG ratio < 1.2. PEG ratio is a valuation metric that compares a company's price-earnings ratio with its projected growth rate. Small, high-growth stocks generally trade at higher PEGs compared to the big-caps. If the PEG ratio is around 1, the company is considered fairly valued. A PEG ratio that is much higher than 1 indicates an overvalued company and a PEG below 1 indicates an undervalued company.
- Five-year Earnings Growth between 15–30%. Very low earnings less than 15% and high earnings growth more than 30% should be avoided as sustaining a high growth-rate over the long term is extremely difficult
- Debt Equity ratio < 35%: If a company's debt levels are excessive, it often proves extremely difficult to raise sufficient cash to finance continued expansion. Without expansion into new markets, corporate growth eventually slows down. Companies with lower debt often have better prospects for future expansion.
- Institutional ownership 5–65% . Percentage institutional ownership is the percentage of outstanding shares that are owned by mutual funds, pension funds and other institutional investors. Most well-known stocks have at least 40 percent institutional ownership, Stocks with a relatively small level of institutional sponsorship offer the best return potential.
- Moderate Dividend yield: Stocks with high dividend yield, called income stocks offer lesser growth potential Nifty stocks have given dividend yield between 0.5% to 3% in last 10 years. Investors looking for reasonable growth should avoid stocks with more than 3% dividend yield.

4.3 Stock Selection Criteria

Stock selection strategies for investors and speculators are different. Investors look for value, growth or income stocks whereas traders hunt for momentum stocks and ride the momentum to make money. The objectives of stock selection criteria for investors are to (1) maximize the total return on investment for the targeted holding period (2) limit risk and (3) maintain an appropriate degree of portfolio diversification. Stock selection criteria for long term investment may include one or more of the following:

(1) Sector and Company Selection

Health of a stock's sector is as important as the performance of the individual stock itself. Even the best stock of a weak sector may often perform poorly. Performance of an industry depends upon its customer base, industry growth, technology, competition, regulation and business cycle etc. Investors should monitor sectors that are nearing the bottom of performance rankings for possible signs of an impending turnaround. Past performance of industry sectors can be seen on www.bseindia.com and nseindia.com. The graphics below shows the relative 1 week, 1 month and 1 year performance of various NSE indices for the period ending 30 April 2020.

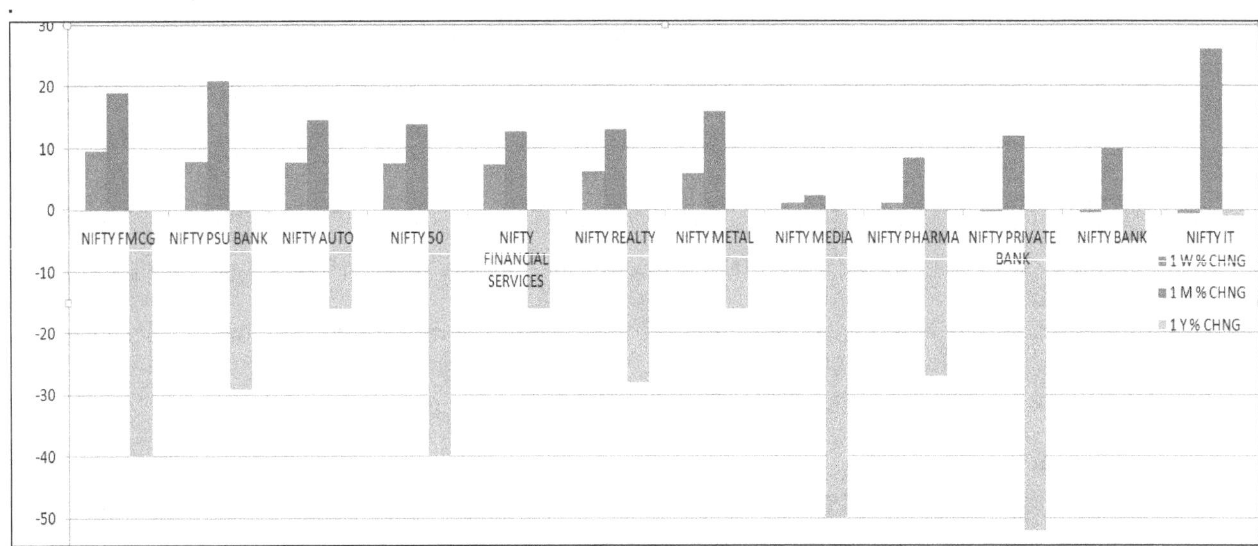

. Fig - Performance of various NSE indices (in %) [source .nseindia.com]

The following observations can be made from this graphic:

1. All sectors have started recovering on the news of opening up of the economy.
2. FMCG, PSU Bank and Auto are the fastest moving sectors on weekly basis.
3. IT, Bank and FMCG are the fastest moving sectors on monthly basis
4. IT, Bank and Auto are the fastest turn around sectors in the past year.

A long term investor can pick up 3-4 sectors as most of the technical indicators are pointing out that the worst of the stock market is over. It is also confirmed by overall market index Nifty 50 which recovered in last one year (ending on 30 April 2020) from -40% to +8% in the last one month. After picking the sectors one should pick at least top two best performing companies in each sector. The purpose of choosing several companies from different sectors is to diversify the portfolio to mitigate risk. The number of companies should not exceed 12 as little benefit of diversification accrues beyond this.

Best Performing Companies within a Sector

After having chosen the following best performing sectors in the past one year (ending on 30 April 2020), Nifty IT, Nifty Bank and Nifty Auto, best performing shares in the past one month or one year period can be chosen from NSE website www1.nseindia.com/live_market/.com. The following table lists top two shares from each sector on the basis of past one month performance for the period ending 30 April 2020:

Table of Best Performing Shares within Sectors

Sector	Company	1-month return %	1-year return %
IT	HCL Tech	30	-54
IT	Infosys	14	-5
Bank	Bandhan bank	22	-56
Bank	Axis Bank	21	-40
Auto	Motherson Sumi	46	-40
Auto	HeroMotocop	39	-14

[Source www1.nseindia.com]

Note: In the above table small and midcap shares have been omitted.

(2) Value Stocks

Value investing, is about spotting companies which are available at a bargain. Value companies are available at less than their intrinsic worth. It requires you to find good companies available at a bargain. Value stocks are available at a bargain. Later when the market recognises their potential, they get rerated and deliver gains. Value investing is not just a logical way of investing in businesses; it's also comparatively safer. You buy stocks at low valuations and this acts as a safety net if the market itself falls. In market declines, expensively valued growth stocks tend to correct heavily and can give investors sleepless nights. Value investing is essentially long-term investing as the realisation of value happens over the long term. This is why a time horizon of at least five years is desirable. According to world's top most investor Warren Buffet, who is a high profile proponent of value investing, "Only buy something that you'd be perfectly happy to hold if the market shut down for 10 years". Amongst other high profile proponents of value investing are Benjamin Graham, Charlie Manger, Christopher H. Browne. Value investors use financial ratios such as PER, PBR, debt-to-equity, PEG and Free Cash Flow (FCF) to discover undervalued stocks. While Value investing delivers good returns in the long run, it has some drawbacks (i) It may be difficult to search good undervalued stocks. It requires thorough research and analysis to detect such stocks,(ii) The stock may not get attraction of investors and over time it may remain subdued or may give negative returns.

The following filers can be used to search value stocks:

* Market cap > Rs 500 Cr,
* Debt : Equity ratio < 1.5,
* Price : book value < 0.9 and
* Return on Net worth in the most recent year > 10%,5 year earnings growth >10%.

Applying these filters some of the most discounted stocks (with low PER and PBR) are found as:
Dalmia Bharat Sugar & Ind, GHCL, Jindal Saw, Gujrat Industries Power, JK Paper, Dhampur Sugar

, Gateway Distriparks, Polyplex Corporation.

(3) Growth Stocks

A growth stock is a share in a company that is anticipated to grow at a rate significantly higher than the average growth of the market. It generates substantial and sustainable positive cash flow and whose revenues and earnings are expected to increase at a faster rate than the average company within the same industry. Growth stocks usually pay smaller dividends, as the company ploughs back profits for capital expansion. Growth stocks trade at a high P/E ratio. These companies have some sort of competitive advantage like economy of scale, new product, a breakthrough patent. These companies generally build some kind of moat to fend the competition. The term economic moat was coined by Warren Buffett. Moat stocks are discussed in a subsequent section. Thomas Rowe Price, Jr. is called "the father of growth investing" because of his work defining and promoting growth investing through his company T. Rowe Price.

The following filters can be used to search growth stocks:
* Market cap = midcap,
* yr Revenue CAGR > 10%,
* 1 yr Revenue growth > 3 yr Revenue CAGR,
* 1 yr PAT growth > 20%,
* Quarterly PAT YoY > 20% and
* Cash from operations (CFO) > Previous yr CFO.

The application of the above filters yields the following stocks: Alembic Pharma, Endurance Technologies, V-Guard, NIIT Ltd, Timken India, Affle (India).

(4) GARP (Growth at Reasonable Price) Stocks

GARP investing is Growth At Reasonable Price, a hybrid system of stock selection. It is a combination of both value and growth investing: it looks for companies that are somewhat undervalued but with solid sustainable growth potential. Followers of this strategy look for companies that are preferred by both value and growth investors alike. Below is a diagram illustrating how the GARP falls between value and growth investing:

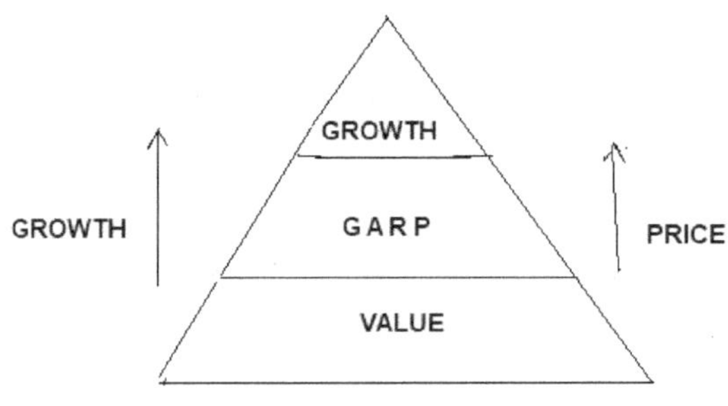

Fig. GARP Investing

The term GARP was popularized by legendary investor Peter Lynch. It is a very popular method of stock selection. Advantages of GARP companies are:
* All weather style

* Companies with strong fundamentals
* Greater stability vis-à-vis Value or Growth stocks

The following filters can be applied to search GARP stocks:
* Market cap > Rs 5000 Cr
* Earnings growth
    At least 20% in the past 5 years,
    At least 20% in the trailing 12 months YoY,
    At least 20% in the last quarter YoY and
* PER < 15.

Application of the above filters results in the following stocks with the highest 5 yr EPS growth:

KEI Ind, Ion Exchange, Transpek Ind, Welspun Corp, Advanced Enzyme Tech, Supreme Petrochem, Satia Ind, Dredging Corp, PNC Infratech. Etc.

(5) Blue Chips

Blue chip stocks are shares of very large companies with a sound reputation and a long history of sound financial performance. They endure during tough market conditions and give high returns in good market conditions. They are often market leaders in their respective industries. They provide consistent annual returns over the long run. Investing in blue chips at reasonable price is one of the simplest methods of wealth creation with limited pain. These are favorites of Institutional investors. Some examples of Indian blue chips are SBI, Bharti Airtel, TCS, Coal India, Reliance Industries, HDFC Bank, GAIL, Sun Pharma, Infosys and ICICI Bank. The following filters can be applied to search blue chip stocks:
* Market cap – Large and mid cap,
* Debt/ Equity ratio < 2,
* Interest coverage ratio > 2,
* %yr average ROE > 20%,
* Annualised earnings growth over the past 5 yr period > 20% and
* PEG < 1.15.

Application of these filters yields the following stocks: Aarti Industries, HPCL, Godrej Consumer Products and Vinati Organics.

(6) Income Stocks

Income stocks also called high dividend yield stocks deliver high dividends resulting in consistent tax free annual income. They provide cushion against stability and generate higher total return. These can be searched by application of the following filters:
* Market cap > Rs 500 Cr,
* Dividend payout ratio < 40% and
* Current dividend yield > 3%

The above filter results in the following high dividend yields with more than 5% dividend yields: Graphite India, Cochin Shipyard, PTC India, Cyient, Himatsinga Sede, NCC and Guj State Fer. Ltd.

(7) Moat Stocks

These are basically companies which primarily operate as a monopoly business. Economic moat is also called competitive advantage. Companies with wide moat have a high market share, operate at high profitability levels, These companies invest predominantly on Product Research and Development, Marketing, Distribution and Sales to keep competition at bay. Key parameters of companies with wider moat have cost advantage over its competitors, high switching cost to customers, large intangible assets, good dealer-service network. These companies have high market capitalisation, high ROCE and good profit growth. According to www.Morningstar.in the following are wide moat companies as on 1st May 2020:

Adani Ports & Special Economic Zone Ltd, Asian Paints Ltd, Astral Poly Technik Ltd, Berger Paints India Ltd, Britannia Industries Ltd, Colgate-Palmolive (India) Ltd, Dabur India Ltd, Divi's Labs, Gillete India, Godrej Consumer Products, Havells India, HDFC Bank, Hindustan Unilever, ICICI Lombard Gen. Insurance Co., ITC, Kotak Mahindra Bank, Marico Ltd, Nestle India, Pi Industries, P&G Hygiene and Health, Reliance Industries, Siemens Ltd, Syngene International Ltd, Tata Consultancy Services Ltd, V-Guard Industries Ltd, Voltas Ltd and Whirlpool of India Ltd.

Moat stocks are discussed in greater detail in an another chapter.

4.4 Selection Criteria of Master Investors

Great investors like O'Neil and Warren Buffet have developed some special stock selection criteria described below:

(1) CAN SLIM

O'Neil's Stock Selection Criteria: CAN SLIM stock selection criteria, a great stock winning strategy has been invented by William O'Neil, one of the greatest investors of all time. As described in Chapter 2, it is an acronym of the following seven components of stock selection:
C = Current quarterly earnings per share
A = Annual earnings per share
N = New things
S = Shares outstanding
L = Leaders
I = Institutional sponsorship
M = General market

The following criteria can be use to find CANSLIM stocks:
- Expected quarterly EPS > (1.25*EPS latest quarter) AND
- Average Earnings 5Year >24 AND
- Current price > High price * 0.85

The above filter gives the following stocks: Bharti Airtel, Dixon Technology, Dr. Reddy Labs, Lupin and Reliance Industries. (source www.screeneener.in).

O'Neil and followers of his CAN SLIM strategy have generated huge wealth by applying this strategy .Serious readers are advised to refer to his book 'How to Make Money in Stocks' (4th edition, Published by McGraw Hill, 2009).

(2) Warren Buffet Stock Selection Guide

Buffett is a strong proponent of the 'buy and hold' strategy. He does not buy a company's shares for a week, a month or even a year. He likes to remain invested for a very long term. His selection guide is to:

- Look for companies with commanding market shares.
- Make sure that the company has a long history of increasing EPS.
- Ensure that the company has been conservatively financed.
- Assess the management performance by evaluating ROE, ROTC and return on retained earnings.

He applies the following six filters to screen stocks:

Sl	Parameter	Condition
1	ROE, 5-Year Avg	>= 17
2	ROI, 5-Year Avg	>= 17
3	Pre-tax Profit Margin, 5-Year Avg	>= 1.2 * Industry Avg Pre-tax Profit Margin, 5-Year Avg
4	Price/Cash Flow Ratio	>= 0.1 but <= 0.8 * Industry Average Price/Cash Flow Ratio
6	Debt to Equity Ratio	<= 0.8 * Industry Average Debt/Equity Ratio
7	Income per employee	>= 1.1 * Industry Average Income per Employee

(Source: Book 'The Guru Investor' by John P. Reese)

Buffett uses one more filter while identifying companies, market share. He prefers the companies that have an overwhelming market share and are dominant players in their fields. A leading stock research firm www.euitymaster.com applies the following criteria to find Warren Buffet type shares: ROE >= 20, Debt/ Equity <= 0.5, Dividend payout >=20%, PER (trailing)=0-15. Top 10 stocks meeting these criteria are: Coal India, Bajaj Consumer Care, HCL Technology, HeroMotocorp, Sonata Software, CARE Rating, TVS Srichakra, Sun TV, Atul Autoand Hexaware Technologies.

Note - Research stocks

Quality research is the key to success. First, identify an index (like the BSE Sensex or the NSE Nifty) to suit your style, then identify sectors within this index that appeal you most. Next step is to create a significant list of stocks within each such sector. Analyze weekly these stocks technically to monitor trend and reversal patterns. You will also need to find out a particular stock's key levels of support and resistance and significant change in volume. Also study the fundamentals of the companies and try to analyse their quarterly results to decide whether to add, hold or sell stock(s). Also monitor your portfolio periodically and measure its performance relative to the market. Replace duds with growth stocks.

----------OOOOOOOO------------

Chapter 5

EQUITY INVESTMENT STRATEGIES

Success in investing does not correlate with I.Q. once you're above the level of 25. Once you have ordinary intelligence, what you need is the temperament to control the urges that get other people into trouble in investing – Warren Buffett

5.1 Introduction

Stock investing is a tool to achieve your financial goals. Investment objectives fall in the following categories: (i) Income,(ii) Growth,(iii) Growth and Income both and (iv) Active Trading. Investors seeking income expect higher current income with little capital appreciation, those seeking growth expect capital appreciation with little or no current income. Third category of investors desire both capital appreciation and some current income. These three categories of investors are aware of stock market fluctuations and risk. Investment in growth stocks carries higher degree of risk as compared to investment in income stocks. All these investors invest in stocks with a longer time of say 5-10 years. The fourth category of investors perform active trading in the hope of making fast money. They invest for the short time ranging from one day to a few months. They carry the highest risk even of losing the entire capital. They are the most aggressive investors whereas those investing in income stocks are the least aggressive. Trading is somewhat akin to speculation and must be avoided by the novice investors.

Individuals have different investment objectives, risk bearing capacity and skill sets depending on which their strategies of investing in stocks differ. These generally involve a trade off between risk and return. Most investors fall somewhere in between, accepting some risk for the expectation of higher returns.

5.2 Types of Investors and Their Time Horizon

Prior to investment in stocks you must determine your investment objective, risk bearing capacity and time horizon to achieve your financial goal. The following table (Table 5.1) describes the type of investors, their risk bearing capacity and the type of stocks in which they should invest to achieve their financial goals.

Table 5.1- Types of Investors

Type of Investor	Risk Bearing Capacity	Time Horizon	Expected Return	Type of Stocks
Conservative	Low, below average	5-10 years or more	Low	Large cap stocks yielding good dividends
Modest	Average	5-10 years	Average	Mix of mid cap and large cap stocks
Aggressive	Above average	2-5 years	Above average	Mix of mid and small cap stocks
Very aggressive	High	1-2 years	High	High beta (volatile) stocks
Speculator	Very high	One day to a few weeks or months	Very high	High volatile momentum stocks

5.3 Investing Strategies

An investment strategy is a set of rules, heuristics or procedures, designed to guide an investor in selection of stocks and holding them for a definite period for fulfilling of his or her goals and maximization of returns. As described in the previous section, an investor must have proper selection and an exit strategy for his or her stocks, to covert the abstract electronic or paper certificate into cash to meet his or her financial goals. There are basically two types of investing strategies passive and active.

5.4 Passive Investment Strategies

There are two types of passive investing (i) Buy and Hold a stock(s) for long term and (ii) Buying Exchange Traded Index funds (ETF). Another very popular investment strategy is Mutual Fund, a semi active strategy, in which your money is managed by a mutual fund manager.

In buy and hold strategy the investor buys stocks and holds them for a long period of time, regardless of fluctuations in the market. The followers of this strategy actively select stocks with sound fundamentals and expected good earnings growth based on certain criterion discussed in the book elsewhere, but after buying the stock(s), they hold it for long period without bothering for short term price movements and technical indicators. Taxation law also favours this strategy (Withdrawn in budget 2020, but old option still available); as per old tax laws there is no capital gains tax on shares if held for one year or more. Warren Buffett is a big follower of this strategy but he exercises utmost caution in selecting fundamental sound stocks and has built fortune by investing in sound companies at times when they were undervalued. Though there is some evidence favouring holding stocks for long time but in the modern time buy and hold strategy has not been very successful due to high volatility of stock markets. Arguments against the long-term strategy are that (i) investors forsake gains by riding out volatility rather than locking in gains, (ii) they can suffer huge losses in the event of global or domestic market crash and (iii) a high quality of research is necessary in selection of stocks.

A better way of passive investment strategy is investing in Exchange Traded Index funds (ETFs), which involves in buying a piece of the stock market. This is done by buying an index fund like BSE Sensex, Nifty 50, Nifty Junior, BSE 100, BSE 200 or BSE 500 and the like. The investor buys into the general market and is not concerned with the attributes of constituent stocks. As index funds are abstract entities, representing the weighted average of some actively traded stocks, they cannot be directly bought. Instead exchange traded index funds, which mimic the composition of indices, can be easily bought and sold on the market just like stocks. In recent times, ETFs have gained a wider acceptance as financial instruments. ETFs are simple investment products that combine the flexibility of stock investment and the simplicity of equity mutual funds. ETFs trade on the cash market NSE or BSE like any other company stock, and can be bought and sold continuously at market prices. They also offer the advantage of low expense ratio, diversification and tax efficiency. The following are the characteristics of ETFs which makes them suitable for passive investing:

- **No Active Management**: The best part of ETF is, there is no active fund manager who is taking decisions on which stocks to buy and sell. Therefore, the chances of error in human judgment are minimal. These funds just track the predetermined wider market index. The only error is tracking error which is usually very small.
- **Less Risky than Stocks**: Chances of a loss when one is investing in a single stocks is high. But as portfolio of ETF consists of several stocks, hence it gives the advantage of diversification. Hence ETF are less risky than direct stocks.
- **Best Stocks at low cost**: Suppose you want to buy best blue chip stocks. Buy a Nifty or Sensex based index fund or a Bank ETF.
- **Long Term Holding**: There is risk involved when a person is holding stocks for very long term because the business fundamentals of individual stocks may go down with time. But business fundamentals of an index (say Bank Nifty), will remain intact always as index necessarily includes only the best stocks as it keeps on churning the constituents depending on market capitalisation.
- **Low Cost**: As there is no active fund management involved, ETFs are most cost effective for investors.

ETFs are beneficial for investors who find it difficult to analyse and pick stocks for their portfolio. Various mutual funds provide ETF products that attempt to replicate the indices on BSE and NSE. Their returns closely resemble the total returns of the securities represented in the index. ETFs are, in fact, mutual funds managed by a fund manager who tracks their performance in comparison to the index fund. The difference in the ETF and the index fund is called tracking error, which ideally should be zero. ETFs available on NSE and BSE are diverse lot like Equity, Debt, Gold and International Indices ETFs. As the name implies, they replicate the index, debt (bonds), gold and international indices respectively. You cannot buy the entire market but certainly the best performing market or index; that is what international investors do. The following is the list of some popular equity ETFs (see Table 5.2).

Table 5.2 - Some Popular Equity ETFs

Issuer Name	Name	Symbol	Underlying Index
ICICI Prudential AMC	ICICI Prudential Nifty ETF	INIFTY	Nifty 50 Index

Kotak AMC	Kotak Nifty ETF	KOTAKNIFTY	Nifty 50 Index
ICICI Prudential AMC	ICICI Prudential CNX 100 ETF	ICNX100	Nifty 100
Kotak AMC	Kotak Banking ETF	KOTAKBKETF	Nifty Bank
Reliance AMC	R*Shares Banking ETF	RELBANK	Nifty Bank
MotilalOswal AMC	MOSt Shares M100	M100	Nifty Midcap 100
SBI AMC	SBI ETF Nifty Junior	SETFNIFJR	Nifty Next 50
ICICI Prudential AMC	ICICI SENSEX Prudential Exchange Traded Fund	ISENSEX	S&P BSE Sensex
UTI AMC	UTI Sensex ETF	UTISENSETF	S&P BSE Sensex

Active investing is an investment strategy involving ongoing buying and selling actions by the investor depending on the market fluctuations. In essence it is selection of right stock and timing the buy and sell decisions to maximise the profit. Followers of this strategy focus on picking stocks with sound fundamentals and good future earnings growth. The process of selection of stocks is described in the next chapter. After buying the stock(s) they monitor their portfolio periodically. They hold the stocks for long term. If any stock is not performing well, they exit it. Active investing is highly involved, requires constant monitoring. Fundamental Analysis is used to judge the performance of the stocks while Technical Analysis is used to time buy and sell decisions. Popular active investment strategies are: (1) Value and (2) Growth. A mix of these techniques is Growth at Reasonable Price (GARP) stocks.

Value Investing

Value investing is one of the best known stock picking methods. It aims at finding companies trading below their inherent worth. Value investors look for undervalued companies selling at a bargain price given their strong fundamentals - including earnings, dividends, book value, and cash flow. These companies, therefore, have the potential to increase in share price when the market corrects its error in valuation.

Growth Investing

Growth investing is in to contrast it to value investing. Value investors look for stocks that, at this moment, are trading for less than their apparent worth. Growth investors, on the other hand, focus on the future potential of a company, with much less emphasis on its present price. They are primarily concerned with young companies in new technologies with expanding businesses. Unlike value investors, growth investors buy companies that are trading at higher price than their current intrinsic worth but with a high future growth. This is actually a contrarian play with the belief that these companies' intrinsic worth will grow and therefore exceed their current valuations. Most growth companies plough back profits and pay little or no dividend and expand their business by deploying reserves.

GARP Investing

GARP investing, as discussed in the preceding chapter is Growth At Reasonable Price, a hybrid system of stock selection which falls between value and growth investing. Followers of this strategy look for companies that are somewhat undervalued but with solid sustainable growth potential. Picking stocks based on the above strategies have been described in the previous chapter. There are other simpler investment strategies like Rupee-cost Averaging and Mutual Funds, discussed below.

Rupee- cost Averaging

Rupee-cost (commonly called dollar-cost) averaging is the strategy of spreading out your stock or fund purchases, buying at regular intervals and in roughly equal amounts. It can have significant benefit to your portfolio. In other words, when the price of a given stock rises, you will be able to purchase fewer shares and when the price of the stock declines, you will be able to purchase more shares. It smoothens your purchase price over time and helps ensure that you are not putting all your money in at a high point for prices. Rupee-cost averaging can be especially powerful in a bear market, allowing you to buy the dips, or purchase stock at low points when most investors are too afraid to buy. Committing to this strategy means that you will be investing when the market or a stock is down, and that is when you score the best deals. .

Mutual Funds

Mutual fund is a basket of shares, normally 40-50. Mutual fund houses collect cash from willing investors and invest it in share market. These are managed by professional fund managers to give returns according to a predefined benchmark like BSE 200. Like stock market, mutual fund investment carries various market risks. Mutual funds come in many categories, viz., open and close ended, diversified equity, hybrid, balanced, debt, monthly income, thematic, quant funds and ELSS (Equity linked Savings Scheme for tax benefits under section 80C) (withdrawn in 2020 budget but option available with old tax rates).

Diversified or multcap equity mutual fund is considered a better option for consistent returns. They come with both growth and dividend options. Most mutual funds have star ratings on a scale of 5 stars. Higher star rating means consistency of returns over a period of 3 years or more. Just like shares, mutual funds must be monitored periodically (at least annually) for continued holding or otherwise. Dividends from mutual funds are tax exempt as also the capital gains after one year of holding subject to ceiling of gain of Rs1 lakh. One can choose a mutual fund suiting his / her needs and risk bearing capacity. These can be redeemed, any time with a small or no exit load, with the fund house. Most mutual funds charge an exit load of 1% if redeemed within a year of purchase. Mutual funds are more suitable to those investors who do not have tools, skills and time to monitor their portfolio regularly. It is advisable to invest in mutual funds through SIP (Systematic Investment Plan) route to even out fluctuations of the stock market. Mutual funds are dealt in detail in a subsequent chapter.

----------oooooo0----------

Chapter 6

MULTIBAGGER STOCKS

"Great companies to invest are like wonderful castles, surrounded by deep, dangerous moats where the leader inside is an honest and decent person. Preferably, the castle gets its strength from the genius inside; the moat is permanent and acts as a powerful deterrent to those considering an attack; and inside, the leader makes gold but doesn't keep it all for himself. Roughly translated, we like great companies with dominant positions, whose franchise are hard to duplicate and has tremendous staying power or some permanence to it." - *Warren Buffett*

6.1 Introduction

Mutlibaggers are stocks which have the potential to earn multifold returns in a stipulated period of time. A stock that gives returns up to five-fold is called a five bagger, while the one which gives 10-fold returns is called a ten bagger. However, identifying them is not easy; it can be like finding needle in a hay stack. US stock market is full of innumerous examples of mutlibaggers whose price multiplied hundred and even thousand times. In India too we have many examples of mutlibaggers like Dr Reddy's Labs, Infosys Technology, TTK Prestige, Reliance Industries, Hero Honda, Titan Industries, United Spirits, Pantaloon Retail, Asian Paints, just to name a few. Dr Reddy's Lab appreciated by over 600 times the original investment in 1993. Infosys gained over 250 times from 1993 to 2009. This chapter describes the characteristics of multibaggers and their identification.

6.2 Identifying Mutlibaggers

Identification of these stocks is far more difficult than large, reliable stocks. Most people leave picking of these stocks as a matter of luck and a few investors are able to pick them at the right time. But research shows mutlibaggers have common characteristics and trends which can be identified by careful watch and research. There is, however, no fixed formula for identifying multibaggers. Picking these stocks requires detailed understanding of their businesses and a vision to anticipate the future of the companies' businesses. The company should have hidden assets and should be deeply undervalued and unnoticed by the market. Its business model and management must be good. Its products or services must have competitive advantage. The following are important criteria for selection of multibaggers:

1. The company should have a lower equity base. Lower the equity base, higher will be earnings per share (EPS) and valuation of the company
2. The company should have high promoter's holding and lower free float stock and hence the stock price will shoot up if year-on-year and quarter-on-quarter results are good.

3. The stock should be substantially undervalued to have ample room for price appreciation. It should have low Price: Book value.
4. The stock should not be much noticed by market. It should have no holdings by financial institutions and fund managers. This will keep its price down and leave room for appreciation when it comes in limelight and picked by the institutions and fund managers.
5. The company should have strong positive cash flows and a robust business model.
6. The company should have a unique business model like CRISIL, Nestle, VST Industries.
7. The company should be debt free. Major IT companies like TCS are debt free whereas real estate companies operate with huge debt.
8. The company should have exponential business growth opportunities like Titan Industries.
9. The company's product or service should not be easy to copy, offering competitive advantage to the company.
10. The company should be in a good sector in sync with economy.
11. The company should adhere to the required corporate governance norms.
12. The company should have good quality of the management.
13. Promoters of the company should have a good track record and enjoy a strong goodwill.

Investors often have some misconceptions about mutlibaggers. They are not for everyone. Their minimum holding period is 3 to 5 years. They are not well known in the market having low liquidity in their initial stages. Further as no stock is good for ever, companies have a life cycle after which they turn bad. Some good mutlibaggers like Infosys, Pantaloon Retail, Reliance Industries and Zee Telefilms etc. crashed up to 50-70% during the market crash of 2008. The investors should enter the potential mutlibaggers at the right time and sell them immediately when they begin to fall.

6.3 Steps for Generating Multibagger Returns

There are following four steps for generating multibagger returns:

1. *Selecting the right company*: Selection of right company is essential in choosing a multibagger. The company should good quality management with huge growth prospects. It should be in industry which is new or experiencing positive change.
2. *Buying the stock at the right time:* The stock must be bought early in its initial phase when it is undervalued and not in institutional holdings. A good measure of reasonably low price could be PE ratio less than 10   and Price to Book (PB) ratio less than 1.
3. *Holding the stock till the market recognizes its full potential*: Once a potential multibagger is bought, you should continue to hold till it reaches its full potential. It is a matter less of skill but more of attitude. Multibaggers are more volatile than the overall market, you should be prepared to sell the stock quickly in case of market crash.
4. *Sell the stock at the right time:* Selling the stock at the right time is a difficult decision but it is crucial to book profits. Paper profits do not make any sense, they may evaporate anytime with bad company, market or global news. You can follow the following guidelines to sell the stock:

   * When it becomes overvalued, PE and PB ratios become too high, say PER>40 and PBR>10.
   * Market gets overheated, that is, Sensex / Nifty PER crosses 25.
   * The fundamentals of the company have changed for worse.
   * You have a better option to invest your money.

The following are some examples of multibagger stocks. These are presented here to have a look at their trends, their rise and fall.

Ex. 6.1. Look at the weekly chart of TTK Prestige. This stock made an excellent up move since May '09 after coming out of a long term consolation (line AA' in the chart). This upward breakout was confirmed by MACD, Stochastic and fanning out of 20, 50 and 100 period EMAs. MACD gave a sell signal in April '11 (line BB' in the chart) followed by sell signal by Stochastic in Sept '6. The investor buying the stock in May '09 and selling in Sept '11 would have multiplied his/ her wealth by 27 times in just 2 years and 4 months. A strong buy signal was again generated in May '13 by a large bullish engulfing candle formation, MACD and Stochastic coming out of oversold zone (line CC' in the chart). An interesting point to note in the chart is the wide gap between the Sensex and the stock from point A to point B; this gap started converging somewhere in May '10, vanishing completely in April '11 (line BB'). The stock is since then moving roughly in unison with Sensex. A long term investor could have held the stock since May '09, with a handsome gain of over 35 times in a period of just 4 years. Thus an investor using charts and even simple indicators like trend lines, MACD and Stochastics is at an advantage of identifying nearly optimal entry and exit points.

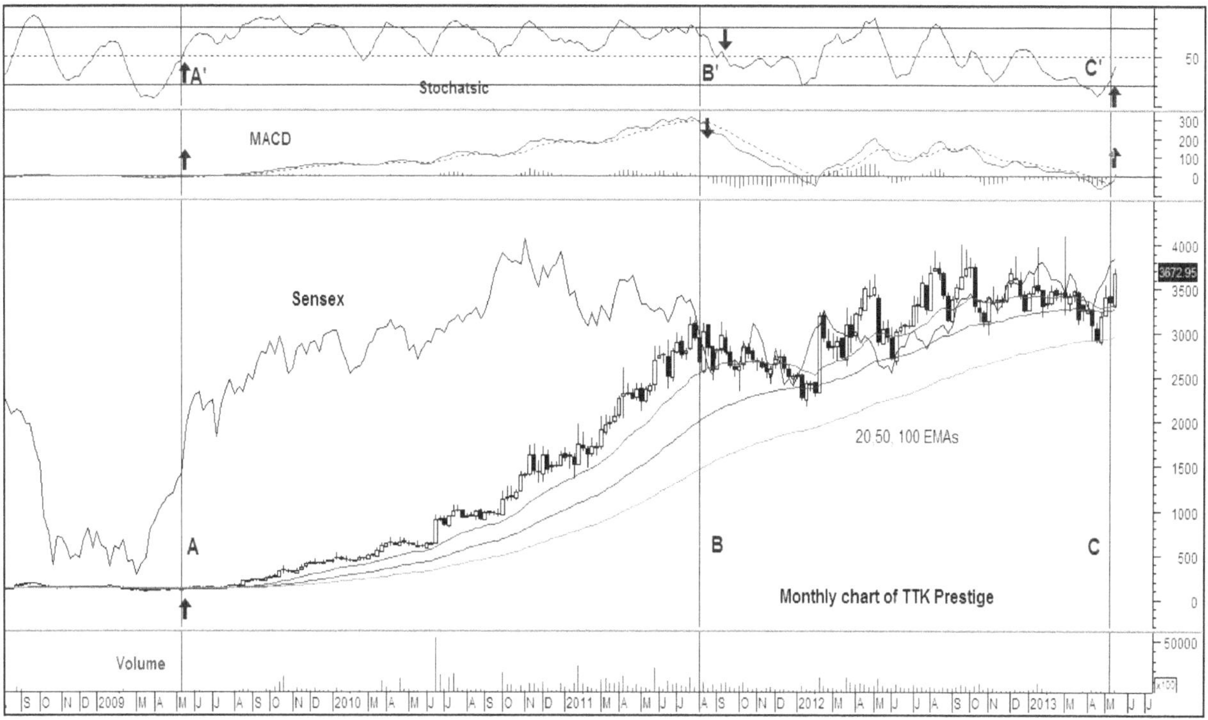

Fig 6.1- Weekly chart of TTK Prestige (Chart created in Metastock)

Ex.2. The monthly chart of Titan Company (Fig 6.2) shows a very interesting example of multibagger stock. Here again the stock was languishing in a long period of consolidation from 1998 to early 2005. It broke out upwards in February 2005 at a price 0f Rs 11 (point A in the chart). This breakout was confirmed by spurt in volume and MACD becoming positive. Since then the stock has seen only upward move as supported by steeper trend lines and positive MACD. By entering even at point A in August 2005 at a price of Rs 30 and holding the stock till February 2020 (point B with the price of 1230), when the price line pierced the trend line CB, one could have simply multiplied wealth 41 fold in 15 years.

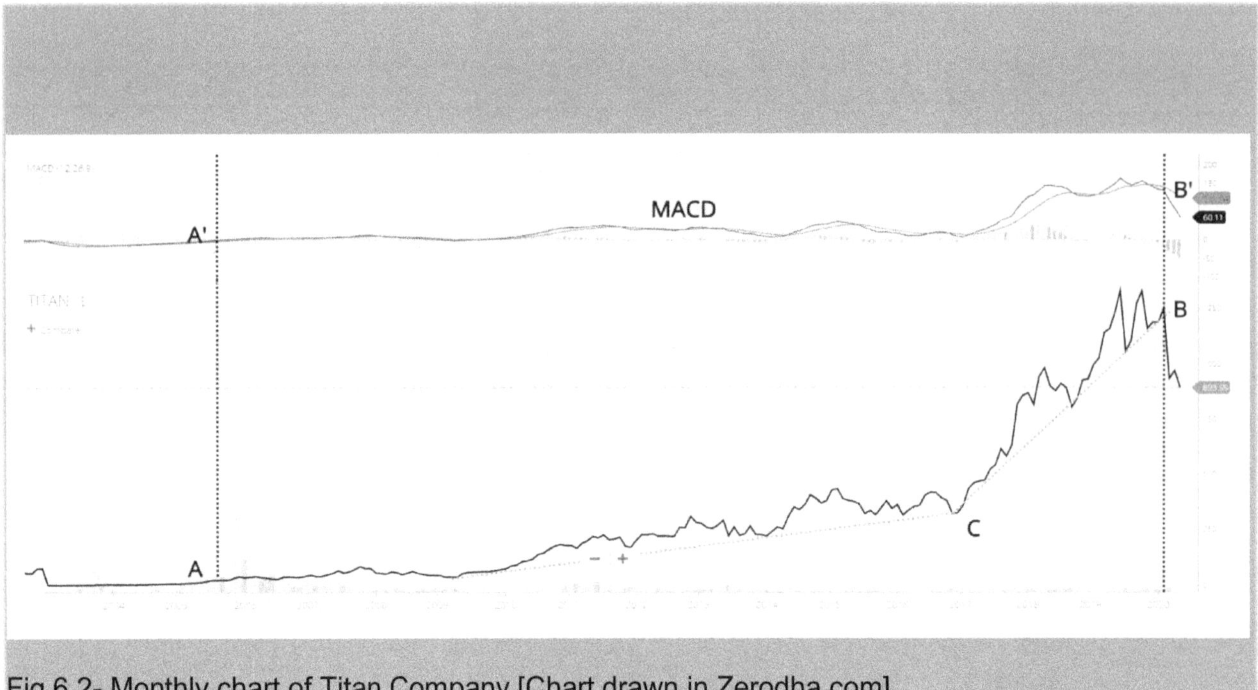

Fig 6.2- Monthly chart of Titan Company.[Chart drawn in Zerodha.com]

Ex.3. The monthly chart of Hero Honda (now Hero Moto Corp) presents another beautiful example of multibagger. The stock broke out in July end 1997 at point A at the price of Rs 62, out of the long congestion zone from 1989. Since then it marched upward till end of January 2013 when it broke the trend line support at a price of Rs 1823 (point B). Your entry at point A and exit at point B would have made a handsome gain of more than 29 times in 15 years. This uptrend is confirmed by the steeper trend lines and positive MACD.

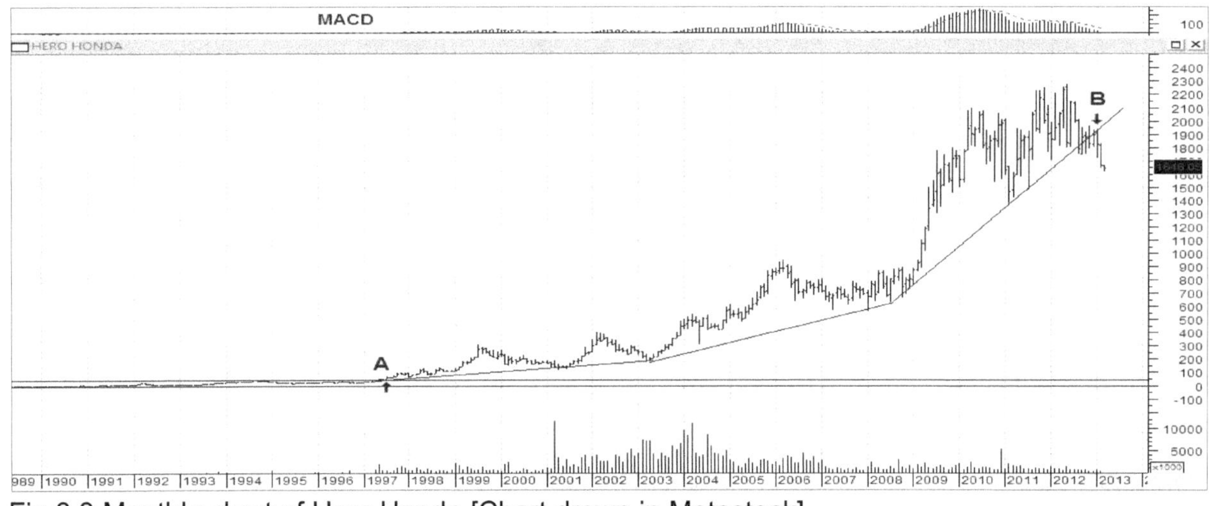

Fig 6.3 Monthly chart of Hero Honda [Chart drawn in Metastock]

Ex.4. Fig. 6.4 shows monthly chart of Asian Paints. The stock gave a breakout at price of Rs 20 in Jan 2004 (point A on the chart) supported by rising MACD. It is since then marching upwards except for a small dip in 2008. Note that MACD remained positive all through with high volume; a conservative investor could have held the stock. The stock is showing a good rise till April 2020 with a price of Rs 1600 (point B on the chart). Selling at Rs 1600, the investor could have a whooping gain of 80 times in a span of 16 years.

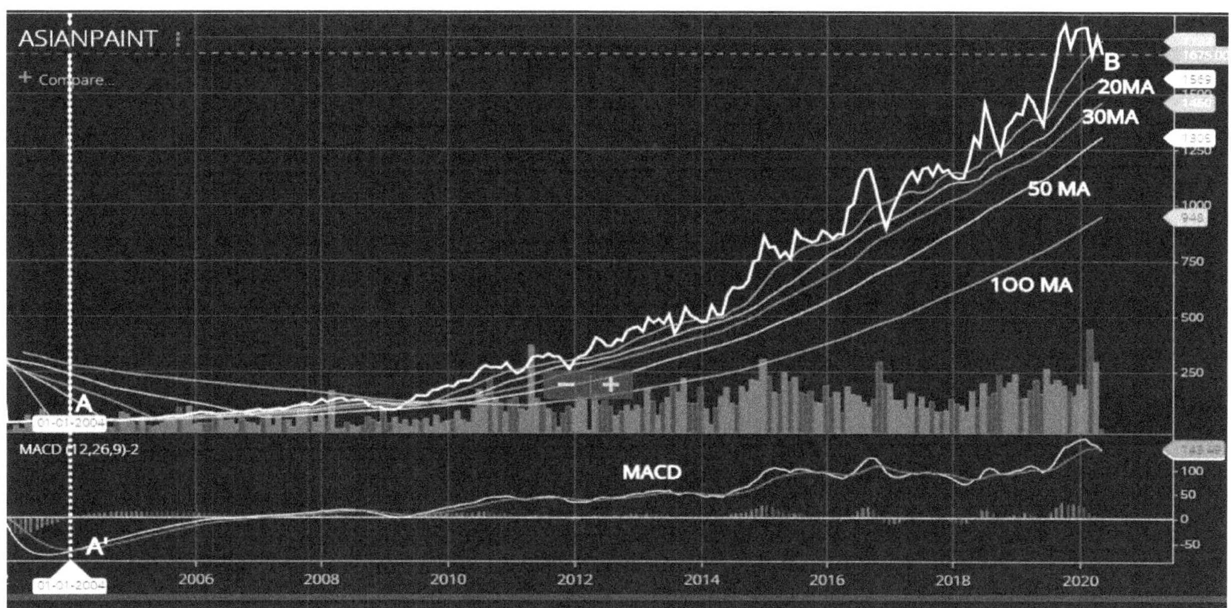

Fig 6.4 Monthly chart of Asian Paints [Chart drawn in Zerodha.com]

6.4 Life Cycle of Multibaggers

Just like the phases of a company multibagger stocks have 3 common phases. They exhibit the following characteristics in these phases:

Phase I: Low liquidity, low trading volume, zero or very few institutional shareholders, cheap valuation, low PER, low PBR and low market capitalization, lack of media coverage, stock price moving in a narrow range.

Phase II: Liquidity increases, average trading volume, moderate valuation and market capitalization, media coverage increases, stock becomes popular in the market, stock price increases significantly.

Phase III: Sharp jump in stock price, price rises vertically, valuations at peak, stock becomes overvalued, price jumps on every good news, high liquidity and trading volume, high institutional participation, high media coverage.

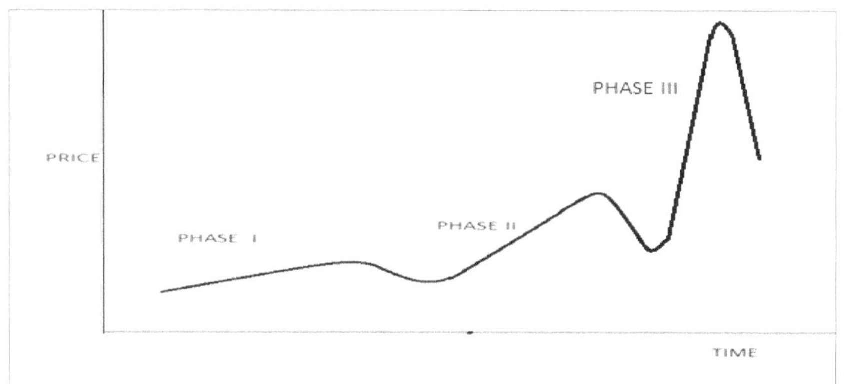

Figure 6.5. Characteristics of multibagger stocks showing various phases

Fig 6.5 shows the above three phases of multibagger stocks. You can notice that the stock corrects for a short time in each phase before making an up move. You can easily recognize these phases in the above charts. You should enter the stock in its first phase and exit in third phase. As illustrated above, charts can assist you in taking the right decision at the right time.

6.5 Risks of Multibagger Stocks

There are some risks in buying future multibagger stocks. The biggest risk is that you are buying stock in companies that are unproven, untested and whose promoters have no proven track record or credibility. You may be proceeding to invest based on rumors and hearsay. You must check whether the claims are correct or not. But if you wait for the claims to be proved, then it might be too late as by that time the share price may have doubled or tripled. If you act on unconfirmed news, then you are taking a big risk if the claims turn out to be false. Another risk is that buying them in the consolidation (first phase) increases your waiting period and locks your money. It would be better to avoid penny stocks with unproven management. You would do better to closely watch future multibagger stocks and buy them at breakout. Just by going on the advice of brokers and market experts may land you in an unwieldy portfolio with most junk stocks.

6.6 Past Multi baggers

Motilal Oswal (www.motilaloswal.com) conducts Wealth Creation study every year. In their 24 Wealth Creation study for the period 2014-2019, the following companies came in the list of top 10 fastest wealth creators during the period 2014-2019 (Table 6.1) and most consistent wealth creators in the 10 year period from 2009 to 2019 (Table 6.2).

Table 6.1 Fastest Wealth Creators during 2014-2019

SI	Name of company	5 year Price CAGR%	Price multiplication
1	Indiabulls Ventures	78	18
2	Bajaj Finance	76	17
3	Bombay Burmah	68	17
4	Aarti Industries	67	13
6	Bajaj Finserv	55	9
7	Sundaram Fasteners	55	9
7	Atul	52	8
8	Rajesh Exports	49	7
9	Honeywell Auto	49	7
10	Britannia Ind	49	7

Table 6.2 Most Consistent Wealth Creators during 2009-2019

Sl	Name of company	10 year price CAGR%	Price multiplication
1	Indusind Bank	49	54
2	Pidilite Ind	40	29
3	Titan Co.	40	29
4	Shree Cement	39	27
5	Asian Paints	34	19
6	Kotak Mahindra Bank	34	19
7	Godrej Consumer	32	16
8	TCS	31	15
9	HDFC Bank	28	12
10	LIC Housing Finance	28	12

You can see in the table of the fastest wealth creators (Table 6.1), 5 year CAGR% ranges from 78% to 49% against BSE Sensex 5 year CAGR of just 14.3%. The companies in table of Fig 6.2 returned CAGR of 49% to 28% in the past 10 year period against Sensex CAGR of 15.3%. What a massive wealth creation!

This wealth creation study also came out with an important conclusion about the key parameters of wealth creating companies. The key valuation indicators of most mutlibaggers are:
1. P/E of less than 10
2. Price/Book of less than 3
3. Price/Sales of 2 or less
4. Payback Ratio* of less than 1

(*Payback is a proprietary ratio of MotilalOswal.com, defined as current market cap divided by estimated profits over the next five years).

6.7 Future Multibaggers

There are several websites and broking firms like www.poweryourtrade, www.moneycontrol.com, www.hjbcapital.in, www.rakesh-jhunjhunwala.in, etc. who advise on selection of future mutibagger stocks. Besides these, there are a number of stock analysts like S. P Tulsian, P. N. Vijay, Ashish Chugh and Aashish Tater etc who track multibagger stocks, also called "Hidden Gems". You may go to their websites to watch and track future multibaggers.

6.8 Economic Moats

"The idea of an economic moat refers to how likely a company is able to keep competitors at bay for an extended period. One of the keys to finding superior long-term investments is buying companies that will be able to stay one step ahead of their competitors."
- Morning Star, a US-based investment firm, which manages a Wide Moat Focus Index

Economic moat can be thought of as a fountainhead of wealth creation. Multibaggers can lead to building economic moats. The term economic moat was popularized by Warren Buffett describing a company's competitive advantage. The wider and more durable a company's competitive advantage, the wider is the moat. And the wider the moat, the better for a company, as it keeps competitors at bay and profits high. In other words, companies with a wide moat will create value for themselves and their shareholders over the long haul, and these are the companies you should focus your attention on.

An economic moat helps a business sustain superior long-term profitability amidst various pulls and pressures (commonly known as Michael Porter's Five Forces in management theory parlance), depicted by the following diagram:

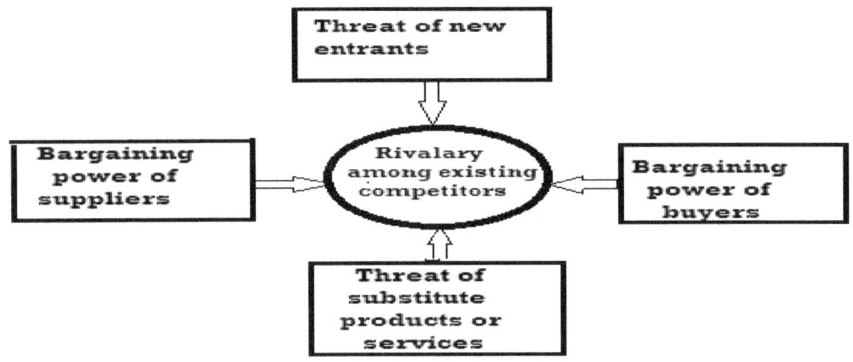

Fig 6.6- Poter's Five Forces of the Industry

Types of Moats: There are four facets/ types of moats:

- Low-Cost Producer or Economies of Scale
- High Switching Costs
- Network Effect
- Intangible Assets

The more types of moats a company can build the better it is for the company.

Low-Cost Producer or Economies of Scale: Companies that can deliver their goods or services at a low cost, typically from economies of scale can undercut their rivals on price. Likewise, companies with low costs can price their products at the same level as competitors, but make a higher profit while doing so. This type of moat creates a significant barrier to entry, since a prohibitively large amount of capital is often required to achieve a size needed to be competitive in a market. Examples of this type of moats are Wal-Mart, Dell Computers. Some of the Indian moats with strong brands are Asian Paints, Hindustan Unilever, Colgate Palmolive, Nestle India, Dabur India, Big Bazaar, Reliance Industries, Dish TV, Sun TV Network.

High Switching Costs:Switching costs are one-time inconveniences or expenses that a customer incurs in order to switch over from one product to another. Companies that make it tough for customers to switch to a competitor enjoy a kind of monopoly and increase prices year after year to deliver hefty profits. The high switching costs lock in the existing customers. The more customers are locked in, the more likely a company can pass along added costs to them without risking customer loss to a competitor. Examples of such moats are Autodesk and Citigroup in USA.

*Network Effect:*The network effect occurs when the value of a particular good or service increases for both new and existing users as more people use that good or service. Examples of such moats are Facebook, ebay, Adobe.

Intangible assets: These are things like patents, basically an explicit monopoly, government licenses that explicitly block competition. Companies with strong brand protected by patents or licenses enjoy pricing power. Pharmaceutical companies with leading brands fall in this category.

Economic Moats and Equity Investing

> *"A truly great business must have an enduring "moat" that protects excellent returns on invested capital."* -Warren Buffett

Equity investing is about forgoing purchasing power today for much higher purchasing power in future, adjusted for inflation and net of taxes. Equity investors, therefore, chase high returns on their investments. In the long run, they can only make as much money and return as the company itself makes. Hence, it pays to invest in companies with formidable Economic Moats, as this is the only way to ensure sustained superior profitability and wealth creation.

Competitive Advantage Period: Economic Moat companies (EMCs) deliver healthy returns over time despite premium valuations. Competitive advantage period (CAP) is the time during which a company generates returns on incremental investment that exceed its cost of capital. When a company earns supernormal return on its invested capital, its business will attract competitors and finally the company will lose its competitive advantage over period of time, thus limiting its CAP. The idea of CAP is graphically presented below (Fig 6.7(a)). Longer the CAP, the better it is for both the company and its investors. WACC is the weighted average cost of capital. A company's WACC is the overall required return on the firm as a whole.

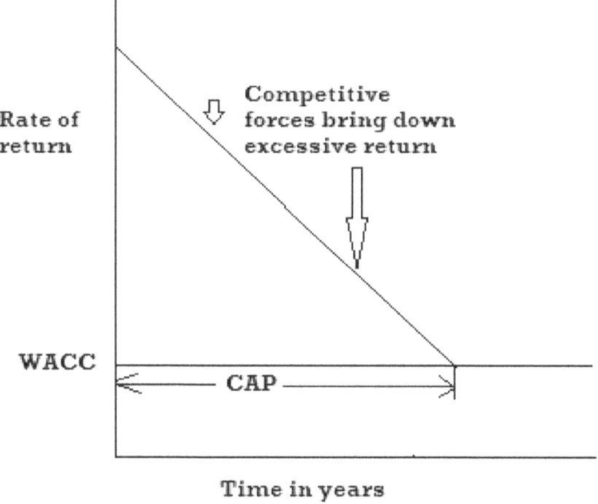

Fig 6.7(a) CAP and Return

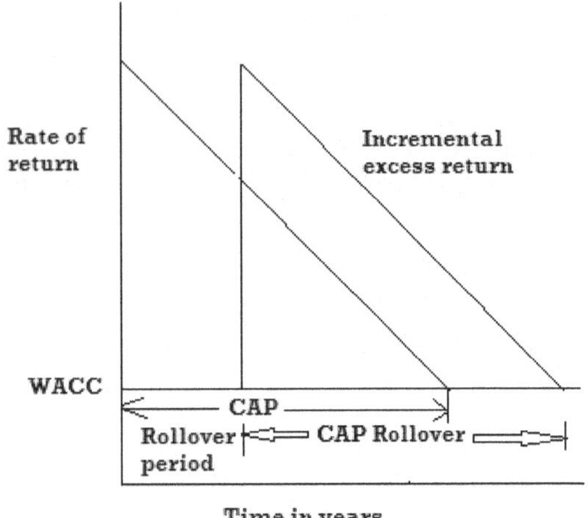

Fig 6.7(b) CAP Rollover

World over, deep economic moats continue to outperform the market much longer than their CAP despite their perennial rich valuations. This is due to the continuous roll-over of their CAP. This is graphically illustrated in Fig 6.7(b).

----------OOOOOOO-----------

Chapter 7

MUTUAL FUNDS

"When it comes to investing, nothing will pay off more than educating yourself.
Do the necessary research, study and analysis before making any investment decision".

7.1 What is a Mutual Fund?

A mutual fund pools money together from thousands of small investors and then its manager buys stocks, bonds or other securities with it with a predetermined mandate. When you contribute money to a fund, you get a stake in all its investments. Mutual funds are considered as one of the best available investments as compared to others they are very cost efficient and also easy to invest in. Thus by pooling money together in a mutual fund, investors can purchase stocks or bonds with much lower trading costs than if they tried to do it on their own. But the biggest advantage of mutual funds is diversification, by minimizing risk & maximizing returns. The collection of stocks, bonds, or other securities in a mutual fund is often referred to as a portfolio. The price of the mutual fund, also known as its net asset value (NAV), is determined by the total value of the securities in the portfolio, divided by the number of the fund's outstanding shares. This price fluctuates based on the value of the securities held by the portfolio at the end of each business day.

7.2 History of Mutual Funds in India

The era of mutual fund in India started in 1963, when Government of India launched Unit Trust of India (UTI). Until 1987, UTI enjoyed a monopoly in the Indian mutual fund market. Then a host of other government-controlled Indian financial companies like State Bank of India, Canara Bank, and Punjab National Bank came up with their own funds. This market was made open to private players in 1993.The first private sector fund to operate in India was Kothari Pioneer, which later merged with Franklin Templeton. Today there are 44 mutual fund houses (Asset Management companies (AMCs)) in the country with Assets Under Management (AUM) equal to Rs 26.75 lakh crore on 31 December 2019.(Source: MutualFundsIndia.com). The biggest AUMs are HDFC, Reliance, ICICI Prudential, Birla Sun Life, UTI, SBI, Franklin Templeton Kotak Mahindra, DSP Blackrock, IDFC, and Tata (In that order). These AUMs operate thousands of mutual fund schemes. There are currently about 2500 mutual funds in February 2020.

7.3 Advantages and Disadvantages of Investing in Mutual Funds

Mutual funds have advantages compared to direct investing in individual securities. These include:

- Increased diversification
- Simplicity
- Daily liquidity
- Professional investment management
- Wide variety to choose from
- Ability to participate in investments that may be available only to large investors
- Service and convenience
- Tax benefits
- Government oversight
- Ease of comparison

Mutual funds have disadvantages as well, which include:
- Fees
- Less control over timing of recognition of gains
- Less predictable income
- No opportunity to customize

7.4 Types of Mutual Funds Schemes

Mutual funds come in variety of flavours. You can choose from over hundreds of mutual funds scheme to choose from. Mutual funds can be classified in the following categories:

(A) By Structure

1. Open - Ended Schemes
An open-end fund is available for subscription all through the year. These do not have a fixed maturity. You can conveniently buy and sell these units at Net Asset Value (NAV) related prices. The key feature of open-end schemes is liquidity.

2. Close - Ended Schemes
These schemes have a pre-specified maturity period. One can invest directly in the scheme at the time of the initial issue and redeem only at the maturity. Some close-ended funds are listed on exchanges; these funds can be bought or sold on exchanges any time at the market rate.

3. Interval Schemes
Interval schemes combine the features of open-ended and close-ended schemes. Units of such schemes may be traded on the stock exchange or may be open for sale or redemption during pre-determined intervals at NAV related prices.

(B) By Nature

1. Equity funds

These funds invest a maximum part of their corpus into equities holdings. The structure of the fund may vary for different schemes and the fund manager's outlook on different stocks. The Equity Funds are sub-classified depending upon their investment objective, as follows:

a) **Diversified Equity Funds**: These are the most popular funds. They invest across all categories and sectors.
b) **Mid-Cap Funds:** These invest only in mid cap stocks.

c) **Sector Specific Funds:** Also called thematic funds investing in specific sectors such as banking, infrastructure, IT, capital goods, FMCG etc. These are riskier than diversified funds as some sectors may be under performing than the market. A beginner should avoid these funds.

d) **Tax Savings Funds:** Equity Linked Savings Schemes (ELSS) offer tax advantage as per section 80C of Income Tax act. An income up to Rs 100,000, clubbed with other investments under section 80C, is exempt from tax. These have a minimum locking period of three years. Due to this lock-in period the fund manager is able to deliver better returns.

e) **Exchange Traded Funds (ETF):** These are essentially Index Funds that are listed and traded on exchanges like stocks. An ETF is a basket of stocks that reflects the composition of an Index, like S&P CNX Nifty or BSE Sensex. The ETF's trading value is based on the net asset value of the underlying stocks that it represents. You can buy and sell it in real-time just like a stock at a price close to actual NAV. Some of popular ETFs are Kotak Sensex, IIFL Nifty, Reliance Gold, BeES Infra, Most NASDAQ 100, MOSt Midcap 100 etc. These are discussed under Passive Investment Strategy in Chapter 5.

Equity investments are meant for a longer time horizon, these funds rank high on the risk-return matrix. They offer best returns in the long period exceeding 5 years.

2. Debt funds

The objective of these Funds is to invest in debt papers. Government authorities, private companies, banks and financial institutions are some of the major issuers of debt papers. By investing in debt instruments, these funds ensure low risk and provide stable income to the investors. Debt funds are further classified as:

a) **Gilt Funds**: Invest their corpus in securities issued by Government, popularly known as Government of India debt papers. These funds carry zero default risk but are associated with Interest Rate risk. These schemes are safer as they invest in papers backed by Government.

b) **Income Funds:** Invest a major portion into various debt instruments such as bonds, corporate debentures and Government securities.

c) **Short Term Plans (STPs)**:These funds are meant for investment horizon for three to six months. These funds primarily invest in short term papers like Certificate of Deposits (CDs) and Commercial Papers (CPs). Some portion of the corpus is also invested in corporate debentures.

d) **Income Plans (MIPs)**:These funds invest maximum of their total corpus in debt instruments while they take minimum exposure in equities. They have the benefit of both equity and debt market and offer regular monthly income. These schemes rank slightly high on the risk-return matrix when compared with other debt schemes.

e) **Liquid Funds**: Also known as Money Market Schemes, these funds provides easy liquidity and preservation of capital. These schemes invest in short-term instruments like Treasury Bills, inter-bank call money market, CPs and CDs. These funds are meant for short-term cash management of corporate houses for an investment horizon of 1day to 3 months. These schemes rank low on risk-return matrix and are considered to be the safest amongst all categories of mutual funds.

3.Hybrid Funds

As the name suggests, these are a mix of both equity and debt funds. They invest 80:20, 70:30, 60:40 or 50:50 in equity and debt in line with pre-defined investment objectives. Debt oriented hybrid funds invest upto 80% in debt whereas equity oriented hybrid funds invest upto 80% in equity.

Balanced funds invest equally, that is, 50:50 in equities and fixed income securities. Equity part provides growth and the debt part provides stability in returns. These offer stable returns in comparison to widely fluctuating returns to diversified equity funds.

4.Index Funds

All the above mentioned funds are actively managed by the fund manager. Their performance is evaluated against pre-specified bench marks like BSE 100, Bankex. There is one more category of passively managed Index funds, which replicate the constituents and performance of some BSE or NSE index. They deliver returns equal to the index with a small tracking error. These funds have been described elsewhere under Exchange Traded Funds.

5.Special Funds

There are special categories of the funds like sector-specific funds, thematic funds and global funds. These are discussed below:

(a) Sector-specific funds

Sector- Specific or Sectoral Funds make investments only in industries of a specific sector such as banking, FMCG, infrastructure, power, pharmaceuticals, petroleum, and technology, media and entertainment. The amount of returns of these funds   depends totally on the performance of the industries of the specified sector. Returns from these funds are highly variable; some sectors perform very well while some funds may be performing badly at a given time.

(b) Thematic Funds

Thematic funds are based on a particular theme which varies from being multi-sector, mufti-economy, international exposure, commodity exposure etc. Its objective is to deliver optimal returns by investing in stocks which qualify to belong within the particular theme. Thematic funds by nature are more prone to risk and volatility. The performance of these funds is dependent on the performance of a particular set sector or a theme, unlike a diversified fund which moves in line with the broader markets. One should take only a limited exposure in these funds. Some examples of thematic funds are BSE TASIS SHARIAH 50, BSE GREENEX, BSE CARBONEX, DSP Black Rock Natural Resources and New Energy Fund, Sundaram Select Thematic Funds, SBI Emerging Business Fund, Sundaram CAPEX Opportunities Fund, MOSt NASDAQ 100 FTF, Birla Sun Life India GenNext Fund, ICICI Prudential Discovery Fund. Some of the consistent performing funds in this category are Birla Sun Life India GenNext Fund, ICICI Prudential Discovery Fund, Reliance Equity Opportunities Fund, SBI Emerging Businesses Fund, Tata Dividend Yield Fund, UTI Opportunities Fund.

(c) Global Funds

A global mutual fund invests in assets around the world including the home country. Global investing opens up your investing horizons to areas you can not normally access. For instance, you could be bullish on gold and would want exposure to gold-mining companies based in Australia. A gold-mining international fund would make the perfect fit for your portfolio. If you are, for instance, bullish on the growth prospects of technology behemoths Apple and Google, a Nasdaq ETF would be the way to go. International diversification, that is, investing in a number of countries around the world reduces country specific risk. The Indian markets have been highly volatile in recent past so diversifying internationally may help reduce the overall risk of your investment portfolio. Fortunately the Indian investor today has an increasing number of options when it comes to investing in foreign assets through mutual funds. There are around a dozen international funds today available to the Indian investor, several of having been launched recently. Some of the leading Indian International funds include Franklin Asian Equity, JP Morgan JF Greater China Equity Off-shore, Mirae Asset China Advantage, HSBC Emerging Markets, Kotak Global Emerging Market, Birla Sun Life International Equity Plan, DSPBR World Energy Fund, Fidelity Global Real Assets, AIG World Gold, Motilal Oswal MOSt Shares NASDAQ-100 ETF, Franklin US Opportunities Fund, DWS Global Agribusiness Fund.

Just as with any other type of mutual fund, there are a variety of international funds with different strategies and investments. The following are some of the Indian global funds with different strategies. Sundaram BNP Paribas Global Advantage Fund invests not just in stocks from Asia, Europe and Latin America but also in real estate and commodities. Similarly the Tata Indo Global Infrastructure Fund invests around a third of its money in international infrastructure companies. Some global funds invest in 'fund of funds' which means that the Indian mutual fund will invest in a foreign mutual fund instead of investing directly in international stocks. This reduces transactions costs and makes use of international investment expertise. For example the DSP Merrill Lynch World Gold Fund (an Indian mutual fund scheme) invests in the Merrill Lynch World Gold Fund. Some funds due to tax advantage, invest at least 65 per cent of their assets domestically. An example of this type of fund is ABN Amro's China-India Fund which invests up to 35 per cent of its assets in Chinese stocks. International funds have some disadvantages like these being new areas do not have much of track record, change in foreign exchange rates and country specific risk.

(d) Growth and Dividend Options

Most of the funds come in two variations; Growth and Dividend. In dividend option dividend is paid in cash and NAV is decreased by this amount whereas in growth option the dividend is reinvested and NAV swells over time. Each option has its benefits and drawbacks. It is for the investor to decide whether he wants periodic income or through capital appreciation in the NAV? Investors who would like to receive periodic income should opt for the dividend option. Those planning to build a corpus for the long-term on the back of compounding should opt for the growth option. Of course, there are tax implications on both options so tax-efficiency also counts. Investments like the tax-saving mutual fund (ELSS) are illiquid due to the mandatory lock-in period of 3 years. The dividend option might also prove useful for risk-averse investors. With the dividend option, investors automatically book profits as mutual funds are usually quick to respond with dividend declarations during stock market upturns.

7.5 Performance Metrics

Performance and volatility of funds are measured by the following parameters:

Alpha (α): Alpha is a measure of a fund's performance on a risk-adjusted basis. The excess return of the investment relative to the return of the benchmark index is its 'Alpha'. A positive Alpha of 1.0 means that the fund has outperformed its benchmark index by 1%. Similarly a negative Alpha would indicate an underperformance of 1%. Likewise if a fund has underperformed its benchmark index by 2% in a year, its Alpha value will be 2. The more positive is the value of Alpha, the better it is.

Beta: Beta, or "beta coefficient," is a measure of the volatility, or systematic risk, of a security or a portfolio in comparison to the market as a whole. A beta of 1.0 indicates that the fund's price will move in step with the market. A beta of less than 1.0 indicates that the investment will be less volatile than the market, and, correspondingly, a beta of more than 1.0 indicates that the fund's price will be more volatile than the market. For example, a fund with beta of 1.2 will be 20% more volatile than the market. Conservative investors looking to preserve capital should focus on securities and fund portfolios with low beta, whereas those willing to take more risk in search of higher returns should go for high beta funds.

R-Squared: R-squared is a measure of the percentage of a fund's performance in comparison to its benchmark A mutual fund with an R-squared of 0 has no correlation to its benchmark at all whereas a mutual fund with an R-squared of 100 matches the performance of its benchmark precisely. .A fund with an R-squared value between 85 and 100 has a performance record that is closely correlated to the index. Professionally managed funds have higher R-squared value as they outperform the index.

Standard Deviation: Standard deviation measures the dispersion of data from its mean. In case of mutual funds, the standard deviation is deviation from the expected returns based on its historical performance. Standard deviation is the risk factor of the portfolio and is indicative of the volatility of the fund. A lower standard deviation implies less fluctuation in returns.

Sharpe Ratio: This ratio measures risk-adjusted performance. It is calculated by subtracting the risk-free rate of return (Government Bond) from the fund's rate of return and dividing the result by the fund's standard deviation. The higher a fund's Sharpe ratio, the better is its risk-adjusted performance. Share Ratio is used to find the best performing fund in comparison to other funds.

Treynor Ratio: It is similar to Sharpe Ratio, the only difference being that Treynor Ratio uses 'Beta' to measure unpredictability in place of standard deviation.

Sortino Ratio: It is an improvement over Sharpe ratio that it uses only downwards volatility in calculation of standard deviation without penalizing the fund's performance for upward price changes.

7.6 Tax Benefits on Investment in Mutual Funds

Investment in mutual funds enjoys the following income tax benefits as per Income Tax act (old):

(1) 100% Income Tax exemption on all Mutual Fund dividends
(2) Equity Funds - Long term capital gain is exempt from tax. Short term capital gain is taxed at 15%. Long term for the purpose of tax is one year or more, as per current tax laws.
(3) Debt Funds - Short term capital gains is taxed as per the slab rates applicable to you. long term capital gains tax is lower of - 10% on the capital gains without factoring indexation benefit and 20% on the capital gains after factoring indexation benefit.

7.7 How to Choose Best Mutual Fund?

Once you have decided your investment objectives, you can pick one of the best performing mutual funds or you can pick a star rated fund. Many websites like www.moneycontrol.com, www.valurreseachoneline.com, mutualfundsindia.com, www.morningstar.in, www.livemint.com provide filters/ screeners for selecting the best performing fund. For example in www.moneycontrol.com you can search top performing funds in the following categories and sub categories:

- Equity: Large cap, Small and Mid-cap, Diversified Equity
- Equity Thematic: Infra, ELSS, Index
- Debt: Long Term, Short Term, Ultra Short, GILT
- Hybrid: Balanced, MIP (Monthly Income Plan) (aggressive, conservative)
- Money Market: Liquid

This search results in CRISIL rank, 6 months, 1 year and 3 year returns for each fund. Alternatively you can search funds from dozens of fund families and categories. After narrowing down search to a particular fund, you can view its historical chart. You can further check its performance with its benchmark index and also compare its performance with four other funds in the same or other category for a period of 1 month to 5 years. A special feature of this website is an analog Mutual Fund Meter with indicates funds rating in the following categories: Not rated, Relatively weak, Blow average, Average, Good and Very good in colours ranging from red to green.

CRISIL Mutual Fund Ranking: CRISIL Mutual Fund Ranking is the relative ranking of mutual fund schemes within a peer group. The basic criteria for inclusion in the ranking universe are three-year NAV history (one-year for liquid, ultra short-term debt, short term income and index funds, and five years for consistent performers), Superior Return Score , Mean Return and Volatility, Downside Risk Probability, Portfolio Concentration Analysis, Liquidity Analysis, Asset Quality, Asset Size etc. Category Interpretation is given below:

* CRISIL Fund Rank 1 -Very Good performance in the category (Top 10 percentile of universe)
* CRISIL Fund Rank 2 -Good performance in the category
* CRISIL Fund Rank 3 -Average performance in the category
* CRISIL Fund Rank 4 -Below average performance in the category
* CRISIL Fund Rank 5 -Relatively weak performance in the category

The website www.vaueresearchonline.com gives very exhaustive information about any fund. You can view its snap shot with risk and return grades, performance with 1 month to 5 year trailing returns, returns since inception, comparison with category and benchmark index, best and worst period returns with graphics, portfolio and fund details.   This site has a special feature of fund card giving valuable information including Value Research Fund's star rating (see below), detailed information about its past performance, fund analysis and risk analysis with Standard Deviation, Sharpe Ratio, Beta, R-squared and Alpha will be explained later.

Valueresearch fund ranking: Value Research Fund Rating, a Risk-adjusted Rating is composite measure of both returns and risk. It is purely quantitative. It gives a quick summary of how a fund has performed historically relative to its peers. It is determined by subtracting the fund's Risk Score from its Return Score. The resulting number is then assigned according to the following distribution:

★★★★★	Top 10%
★★★★	Next 22.5%
★★★	Middle 35%
★★	Next 22.5%
★	Bottom 10%

The website www.mutualfundindia.com (ICRA online) has a special feature of assigning its own ranks to funds. You can use these rankings to (1) evaluate your current portfolio, (2) track funds and take decisions on sale and purchase of funds and (3) find better stocks.

Another popular website www.morningstar.in has several special features like the famous Morning Star 3,5,10 year and overall Star ratings from one to five stars, the Analysts ratings in five categories, viz., Gold, Silver, Bronze, Neutral and Negative, Morning Star Style Box, 3,5,10 and 15 years performance measures like R-squared, Beta, Alpha and Sharpe Ratio and 3,5,10 and 15 year Volatility measures like Standard Deviation, Sharpe Ratio, Sortino Ratio. These terms are described below:

Star Ratings: Morning Star ratings are based on risk adjusted returns relative to category. 1 star rating means that the fund lies in bottom 10% funds of the category, 2, 3 and 4 stars meaning that it lies in progressively next 22.5%, 35% and 22.5% funds respectively and 5 star funds meaning that it lies in top 10% of category funds.

Analysts Ratings: According to Morning Star, Analysts ratings are based on five key pillars- Process, Performance, People, Parent and Price-which its analysts believe lead to funds that are more likely to outperform over the long term on a risk-adjusted basis. Analysts assign ratings as Gold, Silver, Bronze, Neutral and Negative.

Fund Style Box: The Morningstar Style Box (Trade Mark) is a nine-square box representing the size of the fund, large, mid and small on vertical axis and three styles, value, blend and growth on horizontal axis. Figure 7.1 shows a typical Large Growth fund style. Horizontal axis represents investment style whereas vertical axis represents capitalisation. For example the blue box indicates Large cap Growth fund with low risk. The yellow box is a Midcap Value fund with medium risk.

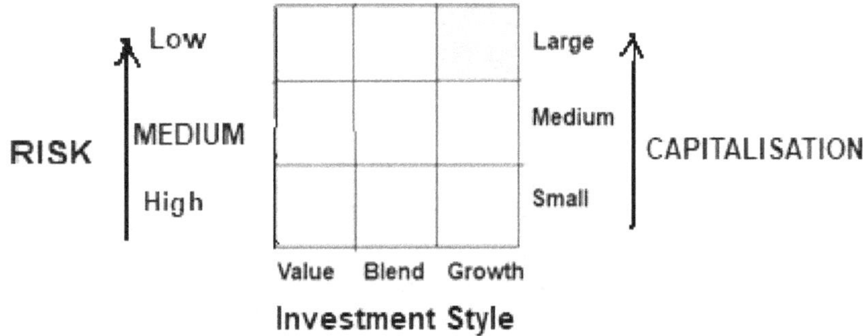

Fig 7.1 Morning Star style box

7.8 Expense Ratio and Loads

Investors in a mutual fund have to pay the fund's expenses and entry and exit loads. AMCs charge investors for investment management and advisory fees, sales/agent commissions and ongoing service fees, legal and audit fees, registrar and transfer agent fees, fund administration expenses, and marketing and selling expenses. All these expenses are together called the Total Expense Ratio (TER) levied as an annual charge on AUM in percentage terms. The NAV of a mutual fund scheme is net of all liabilities including TER, and hence a lower TER results in higher NAV.

There are two kinds of loads on mutual funds; Entry load which is one time charge levied at the time of buying the fund and Exit load charged at the time of exiting a mutual fund scheme. Entry and Exit loads vary from fund to fund. Many mutual funds do not charge exit load if the fund is held for more than a definite period, say, one year. These loads are over and above the TER.

7.9 Buying and Selling Mutual Funds

Once you have your home work right, the next step is to buy the chosen mutual fund(s). Mutual funds can be bought either online or offline. In case you have an online trading account with a broker, you can buy funds on line through the broker; the shares thus bought will be kept in your demat account. You can also buy shares directly from the Assessment Management Company (AMC) in case you already have an online account with it. In case you do not have on line account with your trading broker or AMC, you can buy the mutual fund by filling an application form and submitting it to the broker or Registrar of AMC with the requisite money. The application form and key information about the fund can be had from the broker or downloaded through the web site of AMC or through financial websites like www.moneycontrol.com. Buying through a broker may involve a small commission; brokers charge this commission for guidance in choosing the right mutual fund according to your needs and providing the necessary service.

After having bought a fund, you will need to track its NAV on daily, weekly or even monthly basis. You should track its performance periodically and take appropriate add-on, sell or switch decisions at the quarter end, based on CRISIL ratings / Mutual Fund meter, available on www.moneycontrol.com or based on www.morningstar.in ratings, fund ranking in the category, performance ratios like Alpha, Shrape Ratio etc or the Fund Report Card available on www.valueresearchonline.com or simply based on fund's return in comparison to the market. Long term investors can take a longer view but must churn their portfolios at least once in the year.

Systematic Investment Plan(SIP): A Systematic Investment Plan (SIP) is a vehicle offered by mutual funds to help investors save regularly and beat odds of the market. It is just like a recurring deposit with the post office or bank where you put in a small amount every month. Some mutual funds accept SIPs as low as Rs 100 a month. You can choose a SIP plan for 6 or 12 installments. The main benefit of SIP is that it averages out your purchases over time. With a fixed amount invested every month you buy more units of the fund when the market falls and lesser units when the market moves up; protecting you from losing money with wide fluctuations of the market. Just like SIP there is Systematic Withdrawal Plan (WSP) which enables to sell fund units at regular intervals meeting your financial needs.

7.10 How to Check Performance of a Mutual Fund?

Performance of a mutual fund can be checked on many websites like valueresearchoncoline.com, moneycontrol.com, mutualfundindia.com, amfiindia.com, Morningstar.in. Let us check the performance of Axis Bluechip Growth fund (Direct plan) on valueresearchonline.com. Information about fund is divided in four major heads: Overview, Performance, Portfolio and Fund manager. It is a large cap 5 star fund from the AMC of Axis Mutual Fund. This is a large cap fund that invests in big companies and is suited to conservative investors. The holding period should not be less than 5 years. Performance of this fund with reference to BSE 100 (as on 4 May 2020) is given below:

	1 year	3 year	5 year
Fund	-4.8	8.7	8.5
S&P BSE 100 TRI*	-19.3	0.14	3.5
Rank within category	1/62	1/51	1/49

Note: * TRI stands Total Return Index. It includes dividend paid.

Its risk measures are given in the table given below:

	Standard Deviation	Sharpe Ratio	Sortino Ratio	Beta	Alpha
FUND	16.3	0.36	0.38	0.75	6.7
BSE 100 TRI	20.5	-0.05	-0.05	-	-

Concentration of this fund is as follows: Top 3 sectors = 52%, No. of stocks = 25, Top 10 stocks = 55%, Top 5 stocks = 32%. Its portfolio valuation parameters are : PBR= 4.1, PER = 27.

From the investment perspective Rs 1 lakh (lump sum) invested 3 years before would have grown to Rs 1.28 lakh. A monthly SIP of Rs 10,000 would have grown to Rs 3.67 lakh.

Performance of two or more mutual funds can be compared on several mutual fund websites like www.monycontrol.com, www. valueresearchonine.com, www. livemint.com, Morningstar.in. The following picture is a screen shot showing comparison of the above fund with Mirae Asset Emerging Bluechip Direct.-Growth fund for 3 year period from 12 May 2017 to 11 May 2020.

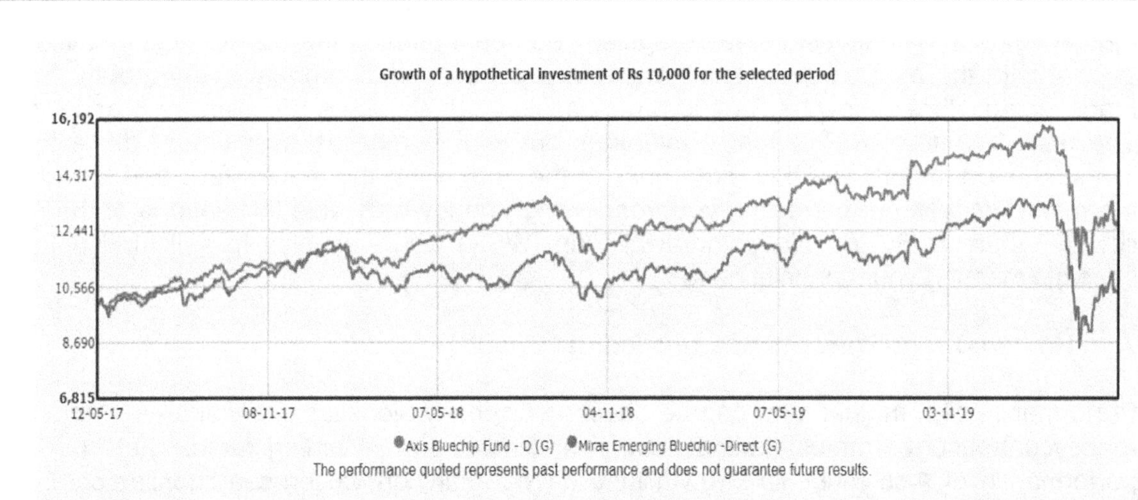

Fig. Comparison of Axis Bluechip and MA Emerging Bluechip funds [Chart plotted in Moneycontrol.com]

It is seen from the above chart that Axis Bluechip Fund has been performing better than Mirae Asset Emerging Bluechip fund.

7.11 Robo Advisors

Robo advisors (Robot+Advisors) are basically algorithm driven advisors that render advice to investors and assist in creating their investment portfolios by taking copious factors into consideration such as the risk tolerance, investment outlay, and the market opportunities. Simply put, they are algorithm-driven (may or may not be intelligent) application that recommends a personalized investment portfolio based on the input from the user. The complexity of robo advisors can vary from a simple algorithm recommending an investment portfolio using very few data points to a sophisticated, AI-driven application using several data points including social media data recommending a highly personalized portfolio for the investor. Robo advisors have taken the Global Wealth Management market by storm in the past decade. Driven by technology, they are easy to use, highly personalized and unlike the traditional wealth advisors, they are affordable by the masses. Robo advisors are estimated to manage roughly $2.2 Trillion of the world's wealth by 2022 Although India is a slow adopter of robo advisors, it is picking up with over 40 players already in the market.

A typical robo advisor collects information from clients through an online survey and then uses the data to offer advice and/or automatically invest client assets. An investment cycle for a new user starts with

* filling an online survey
* creating a trading account
* choosing the portfolio based on robo recommendation
* finally, tracking the performance of the portfolio.

Main advantages of robo advisors over traditional advisors are:

Robo advisor	Traditional advisor
Low cost	Expensive
Low capex	High capex
Real time execution	Slow execution
Data driven	Advisor knowledge driven

Other advantages of robo advisors to the users are:
* Personalized
* Completely digital
* No minimum balance required
* Complete control over the portfolio and choice of investments

In case of mutual fund there is no guarantee of returns, robo advisors recommend investment in a basket of mutual funds to mitigate individual fund's risk. They recommend asset allocation between debt and equity mutual funds, based on the investors age, income, investment goals, time horizon, risk bearing capacity and risk appetite.

Leading Robo advisors in India are: 5Paisa.com, ET Money, Fundsindia, Orowealth, Scripbox, bodhik, Invezta, Goalwise, Arthayanta, Wixifi, Myuniverse, Cion, Groww etc. Some of them are exclusive to Mutual fund investment.

7.12 Wealth Creation with Mutual Funds

The journey to wealth creation starts with setting goals. Your goals should be long-term in nature (5 years and beyond) like children's future planning, buying a dream house, going on a world tour or planning your retirement. Next step is to plan your investments, that is, where to invest with a vision of getting good returns. Equity as an asset class has proven to be one of the most effective investment in combating inflation and providing better returns. They are indeed volatile in the short term but over the long run the volatility too, comes down. Systematic Investment Plan (SIP), in which small amount of fixed or even variable money (variable SIP) is invested every month, is an ideal way to plan your investment in equities. SIP reduces volatility. Just to get an idea of returns from equity look at the following table.

Period	Average rolling returns*
3 years	16.75%
5 years	16.51%
10 years	16.07%

Note * As on 31-01-2019. Based on a SIP of Rs. 10,000 in S&P BSE Sensex on the last day of the month. [Source: Bloomberg]

Systematic investment is the way to go for creating long term wealth. A Systematic Investment Plan (SIP) is a smart and easy way for investing your money in mutual funds in small amounts periodically instead of investing a lump sum amount. This ensures that you don't get carried away by market fluctuations and your investment remains diversified, thus mitigating risks. To summarise benefits of SIP are: (1) Shield from market volatility, this ensures that you are invested in the markets during the highs and the lows and as a result, can make the best of any opportunity that might have otherwise been tough to predict (2) Power of compounding over long term, (3) Flexibility, that is, you can increase or decrease your monthly SIP; you can invest aggressively when the market is low and invest conservatively when the market is high. In mutual funds there is a saying *'Past performance may or may not be sustained in future'*. Today's best performing fund may underperform tomorrow. It is, therefore, prudent to invest your money in 3-4 top ranking funds.

The following funds represent a typical choice of top performing 4/5 star funds from Large cap, Multi cap and Midcap funds, as on 6th may 2020:

Category of Fund	Fund	Crisil Rank	3 year return %*	5 year return %*
Largecap	Axis Bluechip fund- D(G)	5 *	10.5	9.8
Largecap	CR Bluechip Equity fund -D(G)	5 *	7	8.4
Multi cap	CE Equity Diversified fund -D(G)	5 *	4.8	6.1

Multi cap	DSP Equity fund -D(G)	5 *	2.9	7.1
Midcap	Axis Midcap fund -D(G)	5 *	9.2	9.2
Midcap	DSP Midcap fund -D(G)	4 *	0.2	8.6

Note * Annualised, based on monthly SIP [source Moneycontrol.com],

A conservative investor should go for equity oriented hybrid or balanced funds, which invest a maximum of 70% in equity and rest in debt. The debt component acts as a seat belt in case of market turmoil.

7.13 Model Portfolios

Different individuals have different degrees of risk tolerance and needs. The following are 5 model growth portfolios to suit needs of different individuals:

1. **Aggressive Growth:** It has maximum growth potential designed for an aggressive young investors in the age group of 24-30 years. It invests 90% funds in equity and 10% in debt. For the possibility of high return a substantial portion is invested in small and midcap funds and a small portion in large cap funds, due to which it has a high volatility. Minimum time frame is 7 years and above.

2. **Moderate Growth:** Designed for moderate growth for middle aged individuals in the age group of 30-40 years. it is biased towards large cap funds. A small portion is invested in mid cap funds. Minimum time frame is five plus years.

3. **Stable Growth:** It is a balanced portfolio for individuals in the age group of 40-50 years for looking for growth but with limited volatility. It invests in equity oriented hybrid funds with a time frame of minimum three years.

4. **Conservative Growth:** A highly safe portfolio for a conservative investor with a small time frame of one year. It invests in debt oriented hybrid funds with a small component of equity, which is necessary for growth. It is suitable for individuals in the age group of 50-60 years nearing retirement.

5. **Income Portfolio**: It is a highly safe post retirement portfolio for individuals of 60 + age. It provides safe and continuous stream of returns to maintain post retirement income. It invests in a mix of equity and debt oriented hybrid funds.

Table below shows suggested breakup of the above portfolio:

Table: Model Portfolios

Type of portfolio	Large cap	Mid cap	Small cap	Short term debt	Hybrid-equity oriented	Hybrid debt oriented

Aggresive Growth	30%	40%	20%	10%	x	x
Moderate Growth	60%	30%	x	10%	x	x
Stable Growth	x	x	x	x	50:50	x
Conservative Growth	x	x	x	x	x	80:20 (Debt:Equity)
Income	x	x	x	x	50%	50%

-----------------OOOOOOO-------------

Chapter 8

PORTFOLIO CONSTRUCTION

AND MONITORING

"The time of maximum pessimism is the best time to buy and the time of maximum optimism is the best time to sell." *--John Templeton*

8.1 Introduction

The term portfolio refers to any collection of financial assets such as stocks, bonds, and cash. A portfolio is designed according to the investor's risk tolerance, time frame and investment objectives. The objective of a proper asset allocation is maximizing the expected return and minimizing the risk. Diversifying a portfolio across various asset classes minimises the risk. Diversifying assets is about choosing assets which have a low correlation, in other words, this means choosing assets or stocks that do not move together.

8.2 Risk and Return

Risk is the possibility of some unexpected outcome. In a financial world or business you may suddenly gain or lose money. No investment is risk free; some investments like Government bonds carry low risk whereas investment in equity carries higher risk, speculation being the riskiest. There is a direct correlation between risk and return, that is, greater the risk the greater is the return and vice versa. In general, human nature is to avoid taking unnecessary risk, reducing the return. In order to overcome this risk aversion, the investor must be adequately compensated. This calls for tradeoff between risk and return. Taking on some risk is the price of achieving returns; therefore, if you want to make money, you cannot cut out all risk. The goal instead is to find an appropriate balance - one that generates reasonable profit, but still lets you tension free. Risk depends upon several factors like your risk tolerance, years to retirement and your financial needs. Risk management is as important as trying to maximise your returns.

Why Diversify?

A portfolio concentrated in debt instruments, though apparently safe with assured returns poses a bigger risk of inflation in the long run. It will not be able to beat inflation resulting in erosion of principal amount over the long term. This portfolio needs to have a dose of equity to beat the inflation. Despite the volatility of stock market, equity delivers the highest return over a period of 10 or more years. In the short-term the returns from equity and gold are highly variable.

Number of Stocks in the Portfolio

Do not over diversify a portfolio; over diversification becomes even counterproductive by yielding mediocre gains. Research shows that having more than 20 stocks in a portfolio means inclusion of mediocre stocks diluting returns. It also makes monitoring difficult by retail investors. The ideal number is 12-15 stocks with a judicious mix of large, mid and small cap stocks. A global study concluded that about 90% of the maximum benefit of diversification was derived from portfolios of

12 to 18 stocks. Only company specific or systemic risk can be eliminated by diversification, the market or unsystematic risk cannot be reduced by diversification. Risk is generally measured by standard deviation, a measure of volatility. According to the modern portfolio theory (Edwin J. Elton and Martin J. Gruber's book "Modern Portfolio Theory and Investment Analysis"), you will come very close to achieving optimal diversity after adding about the 20th stock to your portfolio and the additional stocks from 20 to 1,000 would reduce the portfolio's risk by about 0.08% (Fig 8.1).

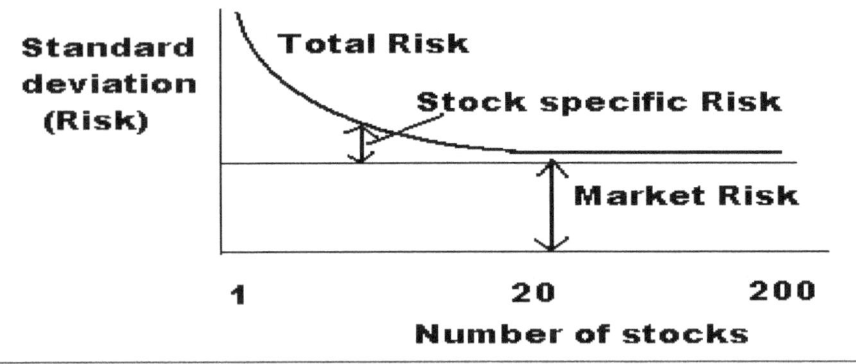

Fig 8.1 Number of Stocks and Risk.

Asset Classes

An asset class is a group of securities that exhibit similar characteristics, behave similarly in the marketplace, and are subject to the same laws and regulations. The main asset classes are real estate, commodities (including gold), equities (stocks), fixed-income (bonds), fixed deposits and cash equivalents (money market instruments):

- **Real Estate**: Investing in property generally involves buying a property directly, or investing in property securities or units in a property fund. Property is usually considered a long term investment. The major advantage of investing in property is appreciation in value coupled with rental income. Its drawback is that it is mostly illiquid.
- **Commodities**: Investing in commodities is owning something physical like property, natural resource commodities and precious metals like gold. This investment is semi liquid.
- **Equities (stocks)**: Buying stock of a company is like owning a piece of it. Its returns are uncertain but the investment is mostly liquid.
- **Fixed Income (debt)**: Investing in debt is lending money to a company or government for interest (government bonds, other types of bonds), deposits in bank or post office. It is mostly a long term investment with guaranteed return and limited liquidity.

Cash and cash equivalents: It is the money in your savings account or in your safe. It also includes investment in money markets which can be enchased on short notice. Money market securities are debt securities that are extremely liquid investments with maturities of less than one year. Treasury bills (T-bills) make up the majority of these types of securities.

These asset classes have varying degree of returns and risks. Figure below compares the risk and potential return of some popular asset classes.

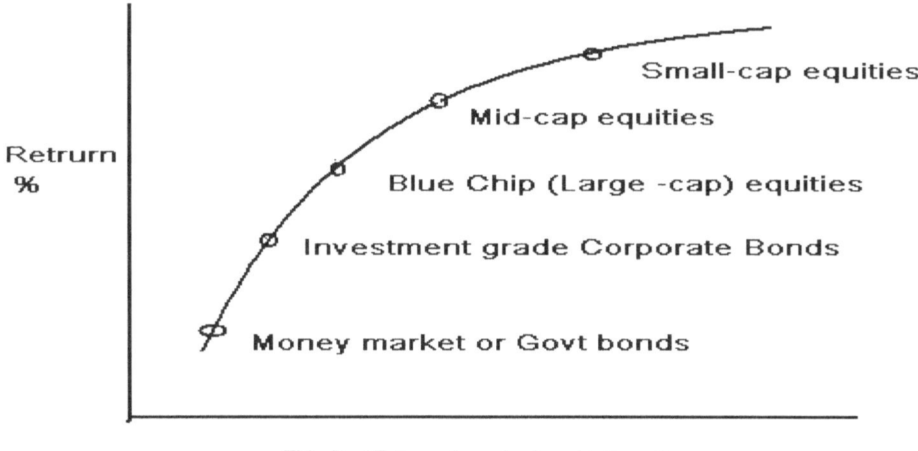

Fig. Return vs Risk of Various Asset Classes

8.3 Portfolio Building

A well-maintained portfolio is vital to an investor's success. As an individual investor, your asset allocation should conform to your personal investment goals and strategies. In other words, your portfolio should meet your future needs for capital and give you peace of mind. You can construct a portfolio aligned to your goals and investment strategies by following a systematic approach. Here are some essential steps to building a profitable portfolio.

Step 1: Determining Your Risk Tolerance and Goals. Ascertaining your individual financial situation and investment goals is the first task in constructing a portfolio. Important items to consider are age, time to retirement, amount of capital to invest and future capital needs. A single college graduate just beginning his or her career and a 55-year-old person planning to retire soon will have different asset allocations. Risk tolerance may vary from low to very high and can be accessed by risk calculators available on many financial websites like www.kotakmutual.com, www.utimf.com, www.moneycontrol.com, www.motilaloswal.com, www.icicidirect.com. Typical goals may be:

- A sum of Rs 15 lakhs for children's education after 5 years;
- A sum of Rs 25 lakhs for children's marriage after 10 years;
- Annual vacation to hill station
- A sum of Rs 200 lakhs to build retirement corpus after 15 years; and
- A sum of Rs 40 lakhs for world tour post retirement.

A second factor to take into account is your risk tolerance. Your current financial situation and your future needs for capital, as well as your risk tolerance, will determine division of your investments among different asset classes.

Step 2. Asset Allocation: Asset allocation refers to the strategy of dividing your total investment portfolio among various asset classes, such as stocks, bonds and money market securities. Weightages to different asset classes are assigned on the basis of your financial status, time for the investment to grow, your financial goals and risk tolerance level. Some typical asset allocations are: Conservative, Moderately conservative, Moderately aggressive, Aggressive and Very aggressive. Table below shows typical weightages of fixed income, equity and cash in these portfolios.

Table - Asset Allocation in different types of Portfolios

Asset type	Conserv-ative	Moderately conservative	Moderately aggressive	Aggressive	Very aggressive
Fixed income security	75%	60%	35%	20%	0-10%
Equity	15%	30%	55%	70%	80-90%
Cash or equivalents	10%	10%	10%	10%	5-10%

Conservative model portfolios generally allocate a large percent of the total portfolio to lower-risk securities such as fixed-income and money market securities. The main goal of a conservative portfolio is to protect the capital. As such, this model is often referred to as capital preservation portfolio. This kind of portfolio is best suited to retired persons who need to preserve their hard earned money as their risk taking capacity is very low, and at the same time they need regular income. A moderately conservative portfolio is ideal for those who wish to preserve a large portion of the portfolio's total value, but are willing to take on a slightly higher amount of risk to get some inflation protection. Moderately aggressive model portfolios are often referred to as balanced portfolios since the asset composition is divided almost equally between fixed-income securities and equities to provide a balance between growth and income. This type of portfolio is ideal for a young person who has recently started earning, has limited liabilities and time on his side for equities to grow. Very aggressive portfolios consist almost entirely of equities. As such, with a very aggressive portfolio, the main goal is aggressive capital growth over a long time horizon.

The above model portfolios suggest only broad guidelines. You will need to fine tune these models depending upon your current liquidity and future capital needs.

Step 3: Monitoring Portfolio: After deciding a particular asset allocation, it is important to conduct periodic portfolio reviews, as the value of the various assets within the portfolio will change, affecting the proportion of each asset class. For example, if you start with a moderately conservative portfolio, the value of the equity portion might increase significantly during the year, making the portfolio riskier. In order to reset your portfolio back to its original state, you will need to rebalance your portfolio by converting some of the equity component into debt. This can be done by following a constant value or constant ratio formula plan, described elsewhere in the book. Constant value plan is a mechanical plan in which fixed sums are allocated to equity and debt in the beginning. When equity portion increases in value, by say 5%, the excess of this amount is moved to debt and vice versa, thus the equity component remains constant all the time. In constant ratio plan the equity to debt ratio is maintained at the pre-decided level. This forces you to trim your equity when it increases in value thus selling when the stock market is high and buy when it is low. You might also need to churn the equity sub portfolio to replace the nonperforming equities or mutual funds with the better performing ones. Good long term gains are possible only with careful monitoring of portfolio, rebalancing and churning its equity portion. There are many equity portfolio monitors through which you can periodically monitor performance of your portfolio and rebalance it. The following section describes some techniques of monitoring the health of equity portfolio.

Monitoring Equity Portfolio: As the equity market fluctuates widely and the performance of an equity portfolio depends on the selection of stocks in the portfolio, it is necessary to periodically monitor the performance of your equity portfolio. This can be done by uploading your portfolio on a website like www.moneycontrol.com, www.etportfolio.com, valueresearchonline.com, www.edelweiss.in. As an example consider ABC portfolio comprising the following stocks, created in Moneycontrol.com.

Table- ABC Portfolio Performance

Sl	Stock	Latest Price	Qua ntity	Inv. Price	Purchas e date	Inv. Amt	Overa ll Gain On 7/5/20	Over all Gain %	Latest Value On 7/5/20
1	Asian Paints	1,594.3	8	1372	1/1/2019	10,976	1778	16.2	12754
2	BPCL	329.6	25	391	1/4/2019	9,775	-1536	-15.7	8239
3	Britannia	2,915.4	3	3040	7/3/2019	9,120	-374	-4.1	8746
4	HDFC	1,703.9	5	1875	7/3/2019	9,375	-856	-9.1	8520
5	HUL	1,992.1	5	1800	1/1/2019	9,000	960	10.7	9960
6	ICICI Bank	336.8	25	396	2/5/2019	9,900	-1481	-15.0	8419
7	Infosys	665.0	15	735	2/5/2019	11,025	-1051	-9.5	9974
8	Jubilant Food	1,544.6	7	1450	1/4/2019	10,150	662	6.5	10812
9	Maruti Suzuki	4,749.3	2	6700	1/4/2019	13,400	-3901	-29.1	9499
10	Reliance	1,507.0	8	1240	1/2/2019	9,920	2136	21.5	12056
11	SBI	170.8	30	301	15/01/2019	9,030	-3908	-43.3	5123
12	Sun Pharma	452.2	25	423	1/2/2019	10,575	730	6.9	11305
	TOTAL					**122,246**	-6841	-5.6	**115406**

[Portfolio created in Moneycontol.com]

It is seen from above table that 5 stocks out of 12 stocks are performing well. SBI, Maruti Suzuki and BPCL are the worst performers. Although all stocks chosen are of good quality, the reason for such a loss is mainly to due to long lockdown from 22 March 2020. Under the circumstances the investor may continue to hold the stocks and review the portfolio sometime after opening of the economy.

A screen shot of health check of the portfolio, showing its weekly, monthly, half-yearly and yearly performance with respect to Sensex, is given below. It is seen that the portfolio is performing better than Sensex. The investor should undertake performance check at monthly, six-monthly or yearly intervals depending on his / her connivance.

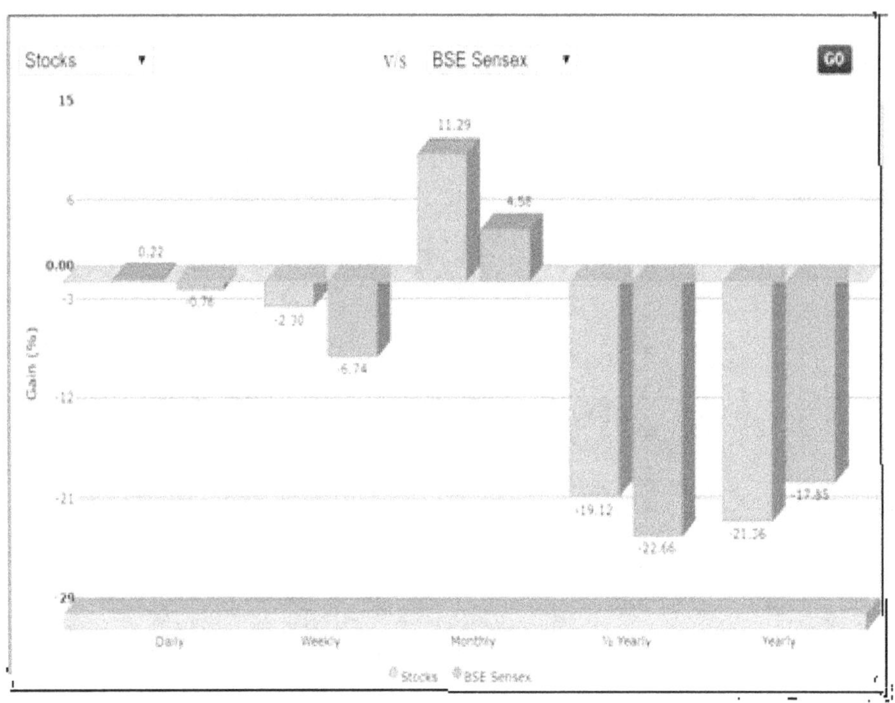

Fig. Health check of ABC portfolio wrt Sensex

You can perform many other checks on the portfolio like industry and sector classification, weights of sectors in the portfolio. Short term and long term trends of the portfolio stocks like very bullish, bullish, neutral, bearish and very bearish.

A tabular analysis of trends of each stock in the portfolio can be done in another software www.in.investing.com. The following table, sorted on 1 year returns, gives a clearer picture.

Table showing performance of stocks of ABC portfolio

Sl	Name	Daily	1 Week	1 Month	YTD	1 Year	3 Years
1	Jubilant Foodworks	-0.7%	-3.9%	9.9%	-6.5%	22.4%	206.1%
2	Hindustan Unilever	-0.6%	-9.0%	-18.8%	3.9%	18.3%	109.3%
3	Reliance Industries	3.5%	3.1%	26.8%	-0.1%	16.4%	128.9%
4	Asian Paints	-0.6%	-9.0%	-0.5%	-10.3%	15.5%	37.2%
5	Britannia Industries	-2.6%	-8.1%	4.9%	-3.9%	9.9%	64.3%
6	Sun Pharma	-0.2%	-2.4%	3.9%	4.9%	3.3%	-28.8%
7	Infosys	0.1%	-6.8%	5.6%	-8.8%	-7.3%	42.1%
8	ICICI Bank	-1.0%	-11.1%	-5.9%	-37.3%	-11.6%	22.7%

9	Housing Development Finance	1.5%	10.9%	9.5%	29.2%	11.6%	11.6%
10	Bharat Petroleum	4.3%	11.0%	-3.8%	33.0%	13.3%	-31.0%
11	Maruti Suzuki	1.9%	11.3%	1.1%	35.5%	28.6%	-28.3%
12	SBI	0.1%	10.3%	-6.6%	48.8%	42.7%	-42.9%

8.4 Portfolio Protection

Stock markets often become highly volatile on some local or global news. There are instances when the index rises or falls heavily. It becomes difficult to protect your portfolio during sudden market crash. A prudent investor can take advantage of such situations. In this plan two portfolios, aggressive and conservative or defensive (debt) are created in the beginning. When the aggressive portfolio rises by a predefined value, say 5%, the investor moves the excess rise (profit) to the conservative portfolio. In case the market falls by the predefined value, he/she moves the short fall amount from the conservative portfolio to the aggressive portfolio. The idea is to keep the value of aggressive portfolio nearly constant under all market conditions. In the ideal case the conservative portfolio is debt portfolio. In this plan the investor keeps the profit in safe haven, and in case of market fall, he/she makes up the portfolio by moving the short fall amount from the conservative portfolio. This is a simple mechanical plan which forces the investor to sell on rise and buy on fall. It nut shell it mimics the basic theory of stock market 'Buy cheap, sell dear.' This plan is called *Constant Value plan*.

There are two more variants of this plan, **Constant Ratio** plan and **Variable Ratio plan**. Under constant ratio pan the investor begins with 1:1 (equal) amount in both aggressive and conservative portfolios. The aim is to the keep the value of the ratio constant under all instances of aggressive portfolio rise or fall by say a predefined number, say 5%. .As an example an investor creates aggressive and conservative portfolios of say Rs 1 lakh each. When the value of aggressive portfolio swells by 5%, that is, it becomes Rs 1,05,000, the investor transfers a part of the excess amount (Rs 2,500) to the conservative portfolio so as to keep the ratio of two portfolios constant at 1:1. Conversely when the market falls and the value of the aggressive portfolio falls by 5% to Rs 95,000, the investor moves a part of shortfall amount (Rs 2500+5000)/2 = Rs 3750 in this case) from the conservative portfolio to the aggressive portfolio so that value of both the portfolios is equal to Rs 98,500.

In Variable Raito plan instead of maintaining a constant rupee amount in stocks or a constant ratio of stocks to bond (conservative portfolio), the investor steadily lowers the aggressive portion of the total portfolio as stock prices rise, and steadily increases the aggressive portion as stock prices fall. In this plan the investor in effect buys more aggressively when stock prices fall and sells the stocks more aggressively in case of market rise.

All these plans are mechanical formula based and thus free from human emotions.

Dynamic Asset Allocation mutual funds follow a strategy similar to the above strategy. They invest in debt and equity instruments based on pre-defined market indicators, such as the Price

Earnings ratio (PER). In dynamic asset allocation, if the PE ratio of a broader index such as S&P BSE 100 goes above a certain level, say 22, the fund would sell a portion of its equity portfolio and increase the portion of its investment in debt securities. On the contrary if PER falls below a certain value, say 15, the fund would buy equity. An investor not having time or tools to manage portfolio can invest in such funds for hassle free investing and automatic protection of his portfolio from big fall in the market albeit at the cost of growth. Some of the best performing Dynamic Asset Allocation funds are Edelweiss Balanced Advantage fund, DSP Dynamic Asset Allocation fund, IDFC Dynamic Asset Allocation fund, L&T Balanced Advantage fund, Nippon India Balanced Advantage fund. [source ETMONEY].

8.5 Life Cycle Investing

Life cycle investing comprises of four phases:

1. Early Savers: These are young persons in the age group 20-29 years. They begin with building assets like luxury personal assets, home goods but have a lot of ambitions.
2. Midlife Savers: These belong to the age group 30-49 years. They accumulate assets like car, home, children appliances. Their major needs are children's education.
3. Transitional Savers: These persons belong to the age group 50-59 years, who are ready to retire and live an active life post retirement. These persons save heavily for retirement. Their needs are children's education and marriage, planning for health care and enjoying vacations through domestic or global tours.
4. Retirees: These are fully retired persons of 65 years or more with limited source of income like pension, interest from bank or postal deposits, rental income etc. and are not as active as in pre-retirement period because of their own or spouse's health problems. Their needs are different like health care, long term care, estate planning.

Portfolios of these phases differ because of the planning and financial needs. In each category there are aggressive, moderate and conservative investors. Table below shows typical their typical asset allocations.

Table - Asset allocation in different phases

Early Savers	Equity%	Fixed income%	Midlife Saver	Equity%	Fixed income%
Aggressive	80	20	Aggressive	70	30
Moderate	70	30	Moderate	60	40
Conservative	60	40	Conservative	50	50
Transitional Retirees	Equity%	Fixed income%	Matured Retirees	Equity%	Fixed income%
Aggressive	60	40	Aggressive	40	60
Moderate	50	50	Moderate	30	70
Conservative	40	60	Conservative	20	80

8.6 Adding Mutual Funds in an Equity Portfolio

Knowledgeable investors buy stocks. Those less-in-the-know, or passive investors prefer to own mutual funds. Mutual funds offer many advantages; they are managed by experts, their performance is measured against a predefined bench mark and they come in many varieties to choose from. But investing doesn't have to be a choice between investing directly in stocks or indirectly through mutual funds. Investors can--and many-- do both. The trick is determining how your portfolio can benefit most from each type of investment. Figuring out your appropriate stock/fund mix is   up to you. Begin by looking for gaps in your portfolio and circle of competence. You may consider investing in thematic or sectoral funds or even emerging market funds. Some funds invest in micro-caps, others invest around the globe, still others focus on markets, such as real estate, that have their own quirks. Serious investors can benefit from new opportunities without having to learn a whole new set of analytical skills. For details on mutual fund types and investments refer to Chapter 7.

How much diversification in mutual funds?: The average diversified mutual fund invests in 40-50 stocks. Two funds from the same category are likely to invest in the same companies. Adding more mutual from the same category will result in duplication of stocks and defeat the very purpose of diversification.   You may choose thematic or sectoral funds if you know which sector of industry is moving with the economy but you have to watch it carefully and exit from it if it goes sour.

-------OOOOOO------

Appendix I

Web Resources

www.moneycontrol.com - leading financial information resource
www.bseindia.com - official website of Bombay Stock Exchange
www.nseindia.com - official website of National stock Exchange
www.sebi.gov.in/ www.sebi.com - official site of Securities and Exchange Board of India
www.crisil.com - Credit rating agency
www.amfiindia.com - official site of Association of Mutual Funds of India
www.morningstar.in - Mutual fund research and rating site
www.valueresearchonline - Mutual fund research and rating site
www.nsdl.co.in- depository services
www.cdslindia.com - depository services
www.business-standard.com - financial information resource
www.livemint.com - financial information resource
www.equitymaster.com - financial information resource
www.economictimes.com - financial information resource
www.myiris.com - financial information resource
www.sify.com/finance - financial information resource
http://in.reuters.com/finance - financial information resource

Appendix II

www.Indiainfoline.com
www.Icicidirect.com
www.Geojit.com
www.Angelbroking.com
www.sharekhan.com
 www.kotaksecurities.com
www.motilaloswal.com
www.religaresecurities.com
www.hdfcsecurities.com
www.karvy.com
www.sbicapsec.com
www.indiabulls.com/securities
www.adityabirlamoney.com
www.axisdirect.com
www.reliancemoney.com
www.ventura1.com
www.smctradeonline.com
www.bonanzaonline.com
www.rathionline.com
www.justtrade.in
www.edelweiss.in
www.zerodha.com
www.rkglobal.co.in
www.unicon.in

For the list of stock brokers registered with SEBI refer to www.sebi.gov.in

Appendix III

Bibliography

1. The Neatest Little Guide to Stock Market Investing, Jason Kelly, Penguin Group, Pearson, 2013
2. Trading Futures for Dummies, Joe Duarte, Wiley, 2008
3. Trading Tools & Tactics; Reading the Mind of the Market, Greg Capra, Wiley Trading,2011
4. Beating the Street, Peter Lynch
5. Learn to Earn: A Beginner's Guide to the Basics of Investing and Business, Peter Lynch
6. The Warren Buffett Way, Robert G. Hagstrom
7. Stock Investing for Dummies, Paul Mladjenovic
8. The Little Book of Common Sense Investing: The Only way to Guarantee Your Fair Share of Stock Market Returns, John C. Bogle
9. Benjamin Graham on Value Investing: Lessons from the Dean of Wall Street, Janet Lowe
10. How to Make Money in Stocks, William O'Neil, Mc Graw Hill, 2009 of Stock Market Returns
11. Security Analysis: Principles and Techniques, Ben Graham and Dave Dodd, Mc Graw Hill
12. Getting Started in Stock Investing and Trading, Michael C. Thomsett, Wiley
13. All About Derivatives, Michael Durbin, Mc Graw Hill
14. Will Teach You to be Rich, Ramit Sethi, Workman Publishing, New York
15. Technical Analysis for Dummies, Barbara Rockefeller, Wiley
16. Trading Options, George Fontanills
17. Day Trading for Dummies, Griffis Epstein
18. Stock Investing for Dummies, Paul Mladjevonic
19. How to Make Money in Stocks, William O'Neil, Mc Graw Hill
20. Options Demystified, Thomas Mc Cafferty
21. All About Stocks, The Easy Way to Get Started, Esme Faerber, Mc Graw Hill
22. Invest to Win, Toni turner and Gordon Scott, Mc Graw Hill
23. Emerging Markets for Dummies, Ann C. Logue, Wiley
24. All About Asset Allocation, Richard A. Ferri, Mc Graw Hill
25. Options for the Stock Investors, James B. Bittman
26. Options as a Strategic Investment. Lawrence G. Mac Millan
27. Getting Started in Stock Investing and Trading, Michael C. Thomsett, Wiley
28. All About Derivatives, Michael Durbin, Ma Graw Hill
29. I will Teach You to be Rich by Ramit Sethi, Workman Publishing, New York
30. How to Make a Fortune in Futures & Options, Ashu Dutt, Vision Books
31. 22 stock Market Trading Secrets, Ashu Dutt, Vision Books
32. 14 Wealth Building Secrets of Value Investing, Ashu Dutt, Vision Books
33. Trader's Guide to Financial Markets and Technical Analysis, Jitendta Yadav, Vision Books
34. The Complete Guide to short Term Trading, Allan Nortcott, Vision Books
35. The Master Swing Trader, Alan S. Farley, Vision Books
36. The Rich Investor, Arjun Parthasarathy, Vision Books
37. Trading the Markets, Sudarshan Sukhani, Vision Books
38. Indian Mutual Funds Handbook, Sundar Sankaran, Vision Books
39. How to Build a Share Portfolio, Rodney Hobson, Vision Books
40. Behavioural Technical Analysis, Paul V. Azzopardi
41. Fundamental Analysis for Investors, Rajat Palat, Vision Books
42. How to Make Money Trading Derivatives, Ashwani Gujral, Vision Books

43. How to Make Money Trading with Charts, Ashwani Gujral, Vision Books
44. Winning with Options, Michael C. Thomsett, Vision Books
45. Profitable Investment in Shares, A Beginner's Guide, SS Greval, Vision Books
46. Futures and Options, R. Mahajan, Vision Books
47. Technical Analysis of Stock Trends, Robert D. Edwards, John Magee and WHC Bassetti, Vision Books
48. Multibaggers, Tejaswy Nanduri, Vision Books
49. Advanced Approaches to Stock Selection, Bruner Ross Paul, Vision Books
50. Balance Sheets, Contents, Analysis and Interpretation, Hemant R. Dani, Vision Books
51. Path to Wealth through Common Stocks , Phlilp Fisher
52. Profitable Elliot Wave Trading Strategies, Rakesh Bansal, Vision books
53. Profitable Short Term Trading Strategies, Rakesh Bansal, Vision books
54. How I Make Money in Trading – and You Can Too!, Vijay Gupta, Vision Books
55. How to Make Money in Intraday Trading, Ashwani Gujral, Vision BooksS
56. How to Make Money Trading Options, , BM Sadekar, Vision Books
57. High Profit Trading Pattern, Kora Reddy, Vision Books
58. How to Make a Fortune through Multibaggers, Dutt and Dutt, Vision Books
59. Shares for Investment and Wealth, Raghu Palat, Vision Books
60. Trading and Technical Analysis Course, M. Jamsandekar, Vision Books

----------0000000-----------

About the Author

Dr. V.K. Jain, a PhD in Electrical Engg., is a Computer Scientist presently working as Director General at HR Group of Institutions, Ghaziabad. He possesses vast experience of teaching Electrical Engg., Computer Science and Management subjects. He was attracted to stock market three decades ago, when he got interested in Technical Analysis. Since then he has been pursuing this subject.

This book is an outcome of his vast experience of the stock market. After seeing people buying useless shares on tips and broker's recommendations and not being able to quit them at the right time thus losing their hard earned money, he was tempted to write this book, explaining complex technical jargon in simple terms and applying principles of technical analysis in a simplified matter, to the real life Indian market situations.

------------O000000---------

www.ingramcontent.com/pod-product-compliance
Lightning Source LLC
Chambersburg PA
CBHW081403130726
47998CB00011B/3053